WITHDRAWN

AN ATLAS OF CURRENT AFFAIRS

AN ATLAS

of

CURRENT AFFAIRS

[SECOND EDITION REVISED]

By J. F. Horrabin

WITH AN INTRODUCTION BY
WALTER P. HALL
Princeton University

TEXT EDITION

NEW YORK · F · S · CROFTS & CO.

1935

Published August 27, 1934
Reprinted Four Times
Second Edition Revised September, 1935

INTRODUCTION

GEOGRAPHY has always been a significant factor in history and politics. In these days when means of communication have made the news of the entire world available for everyday use in teaching contemporary history and politics, a knowledge of widely dispersed areas is essential. Comprehensive atlases have always been and still are expensive luxuries. Maps in textbooks which necessarily attempt to be as inclusive as possible usually become merely confusing. Consequently this compact atlas, simplified yet accurate, creates a tool with which every student of contemporary historical and political movements should provide himself.

In its clarity, accuracy, and brevity it is unique. The omission of insignificant details throws into bold relief the essential geographical facts; the brief notes which face each map offer true and illuminating summaries of contemporary problems; and the inclusion of both maps and explanatory material within the scope of less than two hundred pages is an astonishing feat.

As a matter of contrast in presentation, consider the ordinary text-book map which attempts to show the geographical mix-up resulting from the peace treaties of 1919. The result must lead to a confusing amount of detail and often to inaccuracies. *An*

Atlas of Current Affairs devotes no less than twenty-eight maps to Europe alone, to say nothing of twenty-three descriptive of Asia, and numerous others which illustrate the geographical problems in the Pacific, in Africa, and in South America.

Such a book may be put to numerous uses: (1) for general map tests in which the student is called upon to spot on an outline map (such as is supplied by almost any firm dealing with educational supplies) the data suggested for study; (2) for a day by day discussion of the geographical background of the current assignment; (3) as a supplementary reference text by means of which a student could orient the material in his lectures; (4) for focusing current problems in classes in geography.

The lack of elementary geographical knowledge possessed by college freshmen is astounding. We insist upon a fair command of the English language both written and oral, but geography is seldom if ever stressed before college. If we are to train the youth of America for good citizenship, we should make mandatory a knowledge of geography. If that happy day arrives, books like this will be of great value.

Princeton University
Princeton, N. J.

WALTER P. HALL

PREFACE

No one can read a newspaper intelligently to-day without some background knowledge of world geography. And the ordinary reference atlas, which perforce aims at crowding as many facts as possible into a minimum of space without regard to particular events, is not perhaps the ideal source for such knowledge.

This book is not intended as a substitute for a reference atlas. Its purpose is to be merely a short and simple guide to key facts and key places in the world of to-day. The maps in it are accordingly exercises in "the art of leaving out." Each of them is designed to illustrate a particular point; not to set down every sort and kind of fact about the country or the area with which it deals. The reader is hereby urged to make his own marginal additions as and when his newspaper gives him additional information.

The maps have been grouped in seven main divisions —Europe, the Mediterranean area, the Americas, the Far East, etc. But the world to-day is interdependent; and various cross-references will indicate the impossibility of studying any one problem *in vacuo*.

In common with all students of international affairs I am indebted to the maps and summaries of Dr. I. Bowman's *The New World;* and, for the European section of this book, to Mr. and Mrs. Cole's invaluable *The Intelligent Man's Review of Europe Today.*

I have to express my grateful thanks to Margaret McWilliams for her untiring assistance in collecting and collating material from a mountain of daily and weekly journals.

J. F. H.

CONTENTS

AFRICA

AN ATLAS OF CURRENT AFFAIRS

MAP 1

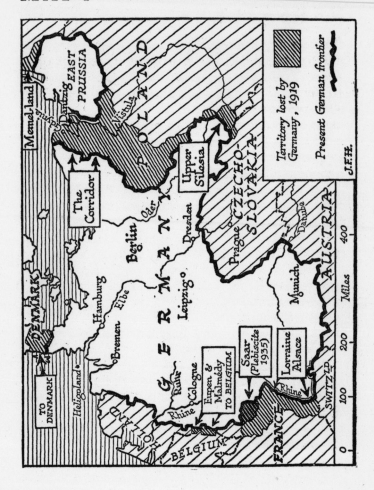

THE TREATY OF VERSAILLES

ANY STUDY of present-day international problems in Europe must begin with the Peace Treaties of 1919. These Treaties made territorial changes in Europe greater than any that had occurred for centuries. They were professedly designed, in accordance with the ideals of President Wilson, to make frontiers coincide more nearly with nationalities. But in so doing they frequently ignored the economic realities of the twentieth-century world.

Let us begin with the Treaty of Versailles, "the corner-stone of the present European political structure."

On her western frontier Germany had to cede the districts of Eupen and Malmédy to Belgium, and the provinces of Alsace and Lorraine to France. In addition, the Saar Basin, bordering on Lorraine, was placed under the administration of a League of Nations Commission for 15 years. (The plebiscite of the inhabitants taken in February 1935 gave a 90.08 per cent vote for return to Germany.)

In the north, Germany ceded part of Schleswig to Denmark (which had been neutral in the war).

On the east, Memel Land, to the north of East Prussia, was at first placed under League of Nations control, but, later (1923), handed by the Allied Powers to Lithuania; the major part of the provinces of West Prussia and Posen went to form part of the new state of Poland; as did also part of Upper Silesia (the exact area of this last being decided by plebiscite later). A further small portion of Silesia was allotted to Czechoslovakia.

MAP 2

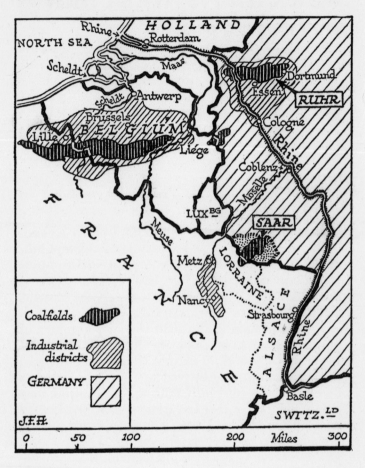

HOLLAND

Rhine
Rotterdam
NORTH SEA
Scheldt
Maas
Dortmund
Essen
RUHR
Scheldt
Antwerp
Cologne
Brussels
BELGIUM
Rhine
Lille
Liége
Coblenz
Moselle
LUX BG
SAAR
Meuse
F R A N C E
Metz
LORRAINE
Nancy
ALSACE
Strasbourg
Rhine
Basle
SWITZ. LD

Coalfields
Industrial districts
GERMANY

J.F.H.

0   50   100   200   Miles   300

4

GERMANY'S WESTERN FRONTIER

THE PROBLEM of Germany's western frontier is essentially the problem of an area economically and geographically a unit, but divided by national frontiers which bear no relation to the basic economic facts of the present day. The Rhine, its tributary the Moselle, and the Meuse and Scheldt rivers are the natural lines of communication in the great coal and iron area of northern France, Belgium, the Ruhr, the Saar and Lorraine. There is no natural frontier anywhere in this region; and, as a matter of fact, of course, frontiers here have been constantly shifting for centuries, long before the days of coal and iron. The Rhine itself is now, on one bank at least, a French river for the 100 miles from Basle to beyond Strasbourg. Then for some 300 miles it is German; while its mouth lies in Holland. The only possible ultimate solution of the problems of this region would seem to be the entire abolition of national frontiers, and its organisation as a single economic area.

MAP 3

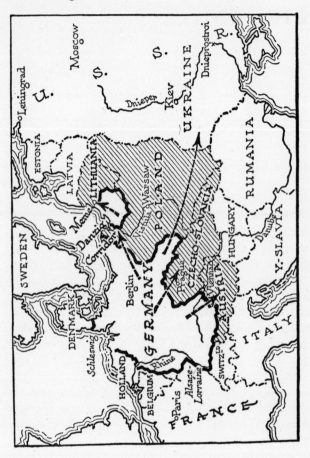

GERMANY'S
NEIGHBOURS

THE declared Nazi aim of uniting under the flag of the Fatherland all the Germans of Central Europe—Hitler himself has spoken vaguely but provocatively of realising Germany's "ideal frontiers"—is inevitably a cause of considerable alarm to Germany's less powerful neighbours. There are German minorities in Holland, Switzerland, Czechoslovakia, Hungary, Rumania, Poland and Lithuania. In addition, of course, Austria is a German state. Nazi propaganda, in some cases backed by organised Nazi parties, has been extensively carried on in many of these countries. The present tendency of German foreign policy is apparently to accept the *status quo* on the Western frontier, while regarding such questions as the position of Memel and Danzig, and the Polish Corridor, as matters for early rectification. Nazi spokesmen have also enlarged upon the possibility of detaching the Ukraine from the U.S.S.R.—whether as a subsidiary German state, or as the price to be paid to Poland for the retrocession of the Corridor to Germany, is not clear.

MAP 4

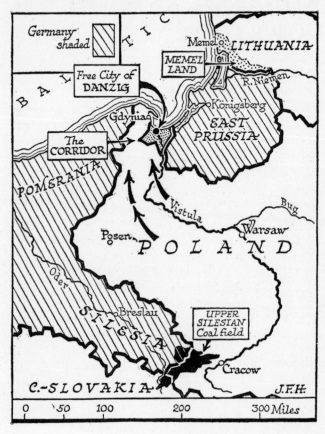

GERMANY'S EASTERN FRONTIER AND THE "CORRIDOR"

THE POLISH "CORRIDOR" is the 50-mile strip of land granted by the Peace Treaties to Poland to give her access to the sea. It cuts off the province of East Prussia from the rest of Germany. The Corridor itself is predominantly Polish in population and the Vistula, which runs through it to the sea, is the main waterway of Poland. "The problem of the Polish Corridor," as a recent writer has acutely remarked, "is not one of right against wrong; it results from a conflict of two principles, of the unity of the seaboard versus the unity of the river-basin. . . . The Poles are the nation of the Vistula and their settlements extend from the sources of the river to its estuary; no other European nation is centred to that extent on one single river" (Professor L. B. Namier, *Manchester Guardian,* Nov., 1933). Danzig, predominantly German, was constituted under the Treaty a Free City, under a League of Nations Commissioner. The local government of the City is at present in the hands of the Nazis. The Poles, in order to avoid using the port, have constructed a new port of their own, Gdynia, which already has the largest trade of any Baltic port.

At the southern end of the eastern German frontier is the Upper Silesian coalfield, the most important part of which (after a plebiscite in 1921) went to Poland.

MAP 5

SWEDEN

Archangel

FINLAND

Reval

Leningrad

ESTONIA

LATVIA

Moscow

Libau

LITHUANIA

U.S.S.R.

E.
PRUSSIA

o Minsk

POLAND

o Kiev
UKRAINE

C. SLOVAKIA

BESSARABIA

HUNGARY

Odessa

RUMANIA

Territory lost
by Russia.
1918-21

J.F.H.

Bosphorus

| 0 | 250 | 500 | 750 Miles |

RUSSIA'S POST-WAR LOSSES

Russia, although not one of the defeated powers, lost very considerable territories in Europe after the war. As a result of the revolution she was not represented at Versailles and the victorious Allies proceeded to confirm the establishment of certain new states created by the Treaty of Brest-Litovsk which, early in 1918, Germany had forced on Russia. In the north, Finland; then the old Baltic Provinces, which became Estonia, Latvia and Lithuania; an extensive area to Poland; and finally (though this was not ceded by the Treaty and has, in fact, never been ratified by Russia),[1] the province of Bessarabia was seized by Rumania. It should be noted that Russia's Baltic coast line (i.e., her direct communication with northern Europe) was thus cut down to the relatively small strip north and west of Leningrad.

[1] The U.S.S.R. has however pledged itself to make no attempt to retake the province by force of arms.

MAP 6

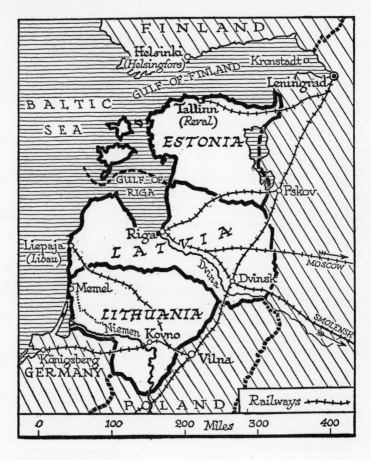

FINLAND

Helsinki
(Helsingfors)

Kronstadt

GULF-OF-FINLAND

Leningrad

BALTIC

SEA

Tallinn
(Reval)

ESTONIA

Pskov

GULF-OF-
RIGA

Riga

LATVIA

Dvina

Dvinsk

MOSCOW

Liepaja
(Libau)

Memel

LITHUANIA

Niemen Kovno

Vilna

SMOLENSK

Königsberg

GERMANY

POLAND

Railways ┼┼┼┼

| 0 | 100 | 200 | Miles | 300 | 400 |

12

THE BALTIC STATES

SINCE the Russian Revolution of 1905 there had been a Separatist Movement in the Russian Baltic provinces of Estonia, Livonia, and Courland. The Czarist Government, intent on the development of the important ports of Reval, Riga and Libau, used every kind of drastic method in its attempt to Russify the provinces. The whole area was in the occupation of the Germans by the beginning of 1918 (when Lenin's Government signed the Treaty of Brest-Litovsk. Anxious to maintain the *cordon sanitaire* against Bolshevism, the Allies confirmed the German creation of the new states of Estonia (the old province of Estonia and the larger half of Livonia); Latvia (the rest of Livonia and the whole of Courland); and Lithuania (the province of Kovno and the greater part of the province of Vilna—see also next map). As the map shows, the ports of Reval and Riga should be (as they once were) the sea outlets and rail heads of very considerable areas of Western Russia.

Since their victory in the Saar plebiscite the German Nazis have concentrated on the re-gaining of Memel (*cf.* map 1). The trial by a Lithuanian court of German Memellanders for alleged treasonable conspiracy has greatly exacerbated relations between Lithuania and Germany. Meantime (September 1934) the three Baltic states unified their foreign policy by a special treaty signed at Geneva.

MAP 7

BALTIC
SEA
Memel
LITHUANIA
Kovno
Niemen
Königsberg
EAST
Dantzig
PRUSSIA
Vilna
(ORIGINALLY
LITHUANIAN)
WHITE
Minsk
RUSSIA
U.
Grodno
Niemen
S.
Vistula
Bug
Brest-
Litovsk
Pinsk
Pripet
Warsaw
S.
P O L A N D
R.
Cracow
POLISH
Lemberg
UKRAINE
UKRAINE
Original Eastern frontier
of Poland (fixed by the
Supreme Council, 1919.)
C-SLOVAKIA
RUMANIA
J.F.H.
0   100   200 M

14

POLAND'S EASTERN FRONTIER

The supreme council at Versailles originally fixed the eastern frontier of Poland on a line (*cf.* map) running roughly north and south from Brest-Litovsk with Polish Ukraine (Eastern Galicia) as an autonomous area under Poland's sovereignty; but in December 1920, after the Russo-Polish war of that year, the frontier was pushed much further eastward by the cession of very considerable additional areas of White Russia and Ukraine to Poland. The original line approximated to the eastern border of the predominantly Polish population. The new area contains large numbers of White Russians and Ukrainians, as well as Jews; and under Pilsudski's régime pogroms took place. Petitions for autonomy for Polish Ukraine (Eastern Galicia) have been presented to the League of Nations but the Council of the League has so far taken no action.

In 1920 also a Polish army raided Lithuania, seizing Vilna, the capital, and adding to Poland the "corridor" of territory north of the Niemen, thus driving a wedge between Lithuania and the U.S.S.R. The Lithuanians have never acquiesced in this particular piece of brigandage and have retaliated by closing the Niemen and the port of Memel to the Poles. The League of Nations has unsuccessfully attempted a solution of the dispute.

MAP 8

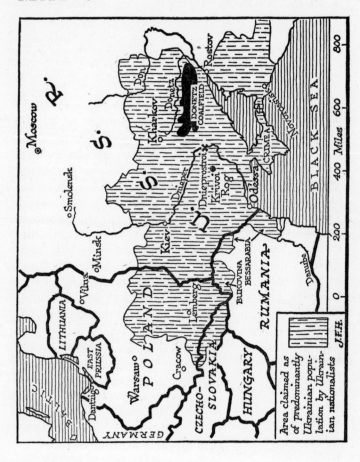

Area claimed as of predominantly Ukrainian population by Ukrainian nationalists

J.F.H.

16

THE UKRAINE

THE UKRAINE, the belt of territory inhabited by the Ukrainians (Ruthenians, or "Little Russians"), extends across south European Russia, eastern Poland and eastern Czechoslovakia, touching also Rumania (Bukovina and parts of Bessarabia). The Russian part of it was constituted an independent state by the Treaty of Brest Litovsk (1918), was overrun by various "white" invaders and "nationalist" leaders after the Russian Revolution, was reconquered by the Red Armies in 1919-20, and in 1923 the Ukrainian Socialist Soviet Republic became a constituent member of the U.S.S.R. It is a vitally important part of the Soviet economic system, including as it does the most fertile agricultural land in Russia—the black earth belt; as well as the great coalfield of Donetz, the ironfield of Krivoi Rog, the important industrial centres of Kiev and Kharkov, and the great electrical generating station of Dneiprostroi (*cf.* maps 54-56). Its coast, with the ports of Odessa, Rostov, and Novorossisk, is Russia's most important seaboard.

During the years of acute food shortage, a counterrevolutionary Separatist movement developed in the Ukraine; but this has now died down and the Ukrainian Nationalist Movement now exists chiefly among circles in Western Europe and in America.

MAP 9

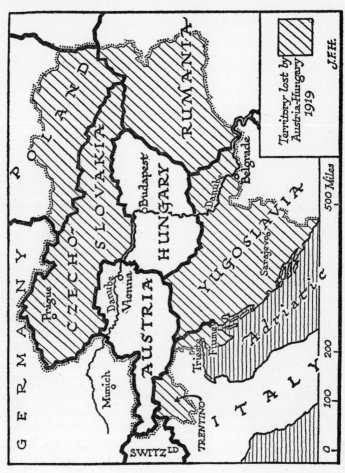

AUSTRIA-HUNGARY'S
WAR LOSSES

Wʜᴇɴ the Austro-Hungarian monarchy was broken up by the 1919 Treaties [1] its population of 51 millions was divided up between seven states. 6½ millions only were left within the frontiers of the new Austria, 8 millions in Hungary. Galicia, north of the Carpathians, went to Poland; Bohemia, Moravia and Northern Hungary formed the new state of Czechoslovakia. Eastern Hungary, with the province of Transylvania, went to Rumania; the Southern Tyrol and Istrian Peninsula to Italy, and Croatia, Dalmatia and Bosnia-Herzegovina were added to Serbia to form the kingdom of the Serbs, Croats and Slovenes, later called Yugo-Slavia. Austria and Hungary thus both became inland states; and the Danube, which for 700 miles of its upper course had been the main artery of a politically unified territory, now flows in that same area through four separate sovereign states.

[1] Treaty of St. Germain with Austria; Treaty of Trianon with Hungary.

MAP 10

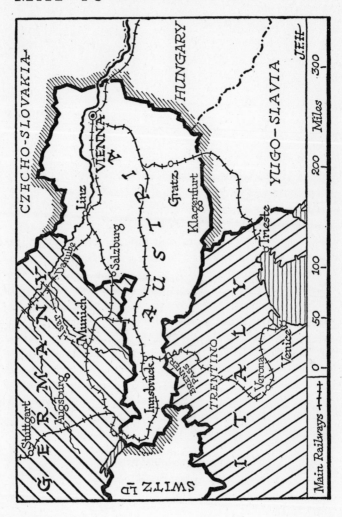

AUSTRIA

Post-War Austria consists of a capital city with a population of two millions, and attached to it a small, mainly mountainous, territory with another 4½ million people. This is an obviously impossible disproportion between a capital city and its country, and the uneconomic character of this treaty-made arrangement has been made clear again and again during the past 15 years, when the League of Nations or various national banks have had to step in to save Austria from complete bankruptcy. The difficulties of the position were accentuated by the fact that the majority of the population of industrial and trading Vienna was militantly Socialist, while the peasants of the countryside were Catholic and Conservative. The population is 97 per cent German-speaking, of the same race, speech and culture as its neighbours of the north in the German Reich.

Austria's geographical position between Nazi Germany and Fascist Italy inevitably lays her open to powerful influences from north and south. Her independence is now fully guaranteed by Britain, France and Italy.

MAP II

THE LITTLE ENTENTE

THREE OF THE STATES created or enlarged by the break-up of the Austro-Hungarian Empire—Czechoslovakia, Yugo-Slavia and Rumania [1]—formed themselves soon after the war into the Little Entente. In February, 1933, they made between themselves a new and more binding Treaty, pledging themselves to follow a common foreign policy, setting up a permanent Council consisting of the three Ministers of Foreign Affairs, and establishing an Economic Council which would aim at the unification of their railways and of uniformity of customs duties. All three states are—naturally—implacably opposed to any revision of the Treaties, and a main point of their foreign policy has always been the prevention of any Hapsburg restoration in Hungary. They are all Danubian countries and, geographically, Hungary (as a glance at the map makes clear) occupies a key position in relation to them, since she controls the strip of the Danube and the main rail lines which link Czechoslovakia in the north with Yugo-Slavia and Rumania in the south.

[1] *Cf.* following maps.

MAP 12

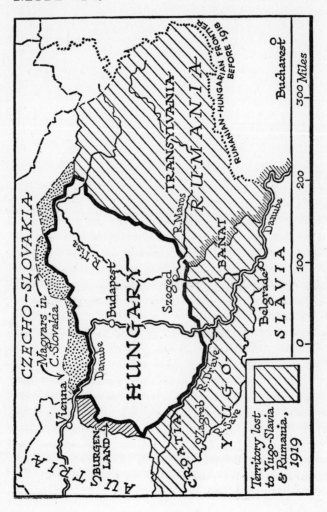

CZECHO-SLOVAKIA

Magyars in C.Slovakia

RUMANIAN-HUNGARIAN FRONTIER BEFORE 1918

TRANSYLVANIA

RUMANIA

R. Maros

BANAT

Vienna

AUSTRIA

Danube

R. Theiss

Budapest

Szeged

HUNGARY

BURGENLAND

Zagreb

R. Drave

R. Save

CROATIA

YUGO-

Belgrade

Danube

SLAVIA

Bucharest

Territory lost
to Yugo-Slavia
& Rumania, 1919

0   100   200   300 Miles

24

HUNGARY

THE NEW HUNGARY is a monarchy with a vacant throne, the nominal head of the Government being a Regent, Admiral Horthy. This is an outward and visible sign of Hungary's refusal to accept the decisions of the 1919 Treaties. Her Government has consistently attacked these Treaties and again and again declared its intention of altering their terms by force whenever opportunity may arise. Nearly a third of the total number of Magyars were left outside the new Hungarian frontiers—in Rumania (Transylvania), along the southern borders of Czechoslovakia, and in Yugo-Slavia (the Banat). The demands of Hungarian spokesmen include, as well as an extension of Hungary's frontiers to bring in the Magyars of Czechoslovakia and the Banat, the setting up of an autonomous Transylvania, and plebiscites to decide the future of the Croats in Yugo-Slavia, the Austrians of the Burgenland and the Ukrainians of eastern Czechoslovakia.

MAP 13

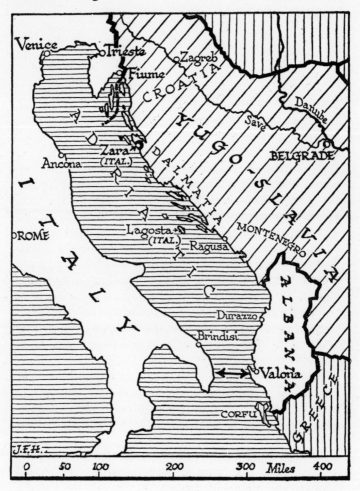

Venice · Trieste · Zagreb · CROATIA · YUGO-SLAVIA · Fiume · Danube · Save · BELGRADE · Ancona · Zara (ITAL.) · DALMATIA · ROME · ITALY · Lagosta (ITAL.) · Ragusa · MONTENEGRO · ADRIATIC · ALBANIA · Durazzo · Brindisi · Valona · GREECE · CORFU

J.F.H.

0	50	100		200		300	Miles	400

ITALY, YUGO-SLAVIA AND THE ADRIATIC

I TALY IS BROUGHT into opposition to the Little Entente from her desire for complete control of the Adriatic and her consequent hostility to Yugo-Slavia development on the Dalmatian coast. By the Treaty of 1919 Italy gained the Austrian port of Trieste and later seized Fiume. The Treaty of Rapallo (1920) gave her the port of Zara and the island of Lagosta. She also exercises a virtual protectorate over Albania, which was made an independent state after the Balkan War of 1913, largely in order to keep Yugo-Slavia (then Serbia) from the Adriatic coast-line which she has since attained. The Treaty of Tirana (1926) gave Italy the right of intervention in Albanian affairs. The harbour of Valona, immediately opposite the heel of the Italian "boot," is obviously of first-class strategic importance to Italy. A Society for the Economic Development of Albania is controlled by Italian banks, and military roads have been constructed right up to the Yugo-Slav frontier. The position of Albania in relation to Italy and the Adriatic Sea may appropriately be compared to that of Cuba in relation to the United States and the Caribbean.

Italian–Yugo-Slav relations have considerably improved since the rapprochement between Italy and France; and Signor Mussolini has recently proposed a commercial treaty between the two countries.

MAP 14

RUMANIA

R.Drave

Danube

Belgrade

R.Save

Fiume

Moravia

Adriatic

Split

Drin

Vardar

ITALY

ALBANIA

GREECE

Salonika

Ægean

Mountains

Railway ++++++

J.F.H.

0   100 Miles 200   300

THE LITTLE ENTENTE:
(i) YUGO-SLAVIA

THE NEW STATE of Yugo-Slavia has realised the old Serbian dream of an Adriatic coast-line; but the advantages of this are severely limited by certain geographical facts. Western Yugo-Slavia is mountainous and there is thus a formidable barrier between the interior of the country and the coast-line. Of the two main railways which cross it, the northern branch leads to Fiume, now in Italian hands, (the Yugo-Slavs have been allotted the suburb of Susak); the southern branch going to Split (Spalato.) The country's main river system, the Danube, and its tributaries, the Save, Drave, and Morava, also lead eastwards, away from the Adriatic. The Drin Valley, a means of access through south central Yugo-Slavia, runs through Albania and hence is blocked by Italian opposition. The Vardar Valley, running south to the Aegean, is closed by Greece's possession of Salonika.

MAP 15

Legend:

- Serbs
- Croats, Bosnians, Dalmatians, Montenegrins
- Slovenes
- Rumanians
- Albanians
- Bulgarians & Macedonians

NATIONALITIES IN YUGO-SLAVIA

Yugo-Slavia, the Kingdom of the Serbs, Croats and Slovenes, was in 1919 formed out of the old Serbia (which had already been extended down the Vardar valley after the Balkan Wars, 1912-13) *plus* the Slavonic provinces of Austria-Hungary (Croatia-Slavonia, Bosnia and Herzegovina) and the Kingdom of Montenegro. From the outset the Serbs tended to regard these other areas as subordinate provinces, to be administered by a centralised government at Belgrade; an attitude resolutely opposed by the National Committees of the ex-Austrian provinces. The Croats in particular—more industrialised and urbanised than the Serbs (they are also Catholics while the Serbs are of the Orthodox Church)—demanded autonomy.

Years of internal struggle were cut short by the late King Alexander's *coup d'état* in 1929, and the establishment of a new constitution based on a specially designed "revised" democracy with only one National party, and the monarch as dictator. The Regency set up after the assassination of Alexander has to face the problem of reconciling Croatian claims with the unity of the Yugo-Slavian state. (See also map 18, Bulgaria, for the Macedonian question.)

31

MAP 16

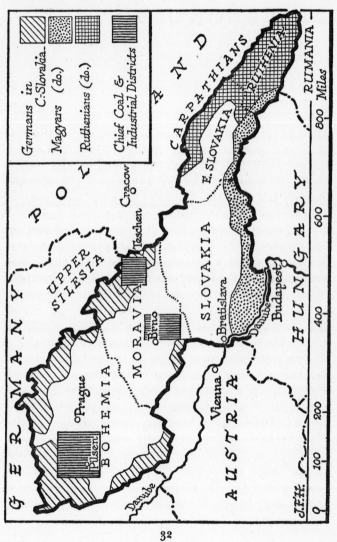

Legend:
- Germans in C.-Slovakia.
- Magyars (do.)
- Ruthenians (do.)
- Chief Coal & Industrial Districts

GERMANY

POLAND

Upper Silesia

Cracow

Teschen

BOHEMIA
Prague
Pilsen

MORAVIA
Brno

Danube

AUSTRIA
Vienna

SLOVAKIA
Bratislava
Danube

E. SLOVAKIA

CARPATHIANS

RUTHENIA

RUMANIA

HUNGARY
Budapest

Danube

J.F.H.

0   100   200   300   400   600   800 Miles

THE LITTLE ENTENTE:
(ii) CZECHOSLOVAKIA

By far the most industrially developed (and demo-cratic) of the three countries of the Little Entente is Czechoslovakia. With the exception of a small district of Upper Silesia ceded by Germany, it is formed entirely out of territory which was formerly part of Austria-Hungary; including, in Bohemia, the most densely-populated region of the Empire. Between 60 and 70 per cent of the total population are Czechs and Slovaks; 20 per cent are Germans (the Nazi Party made sensational gains in the elections of May 1935); while Magyars and Ruthenians make up close on 10 per cent.

The province of Ruthenia (at the extreme east of the country—it is further away from Prague than is Hamburg) is neither Czech nor Slovak, and was added to Czechoslovakia in order to provide territorial con-tact with Rumania, and complete the ring round Hungary. As this area consisted mainly of the great estates of Magyar nobles, its inclusion in Czecho-slovakia forms one of the bitterest complaints of the Hungarian governing class. Its inhabitants are peas-ants, with a quite different standard of living to that of the majority of the workers of the rest of the country.

(*Cf.* map 22 for Czechoslovakia's communications with the sea.)

MAP 17

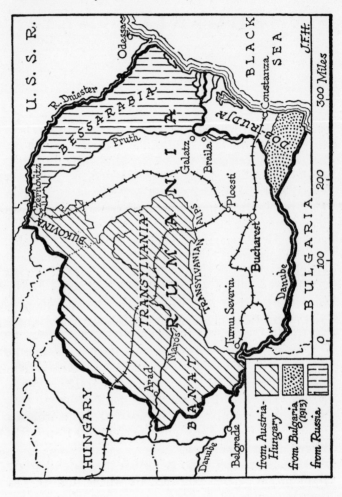

THE LITTLE ENTENTE:
(iii) RUMANIA

R UMANIA, which more than doubled its size and population after the War—and which naturally, therefore, is fervently opposed to any revision of Treaties—is predominantly a nation of peasants. It includes very large racial minorities, including half a million Ukrainians, the same number of Germans and of Jews, more than a million Magyars, over 200,000 Bulgars and nearly the same number of Turks and Tartars. The Ukrainians are for the most part inhabitants of Bessarabia, the Russian province which Rumania seized in 1919 (*cf.* map 5), and of Bukovina, before the War a crown province of Austria. The Magyars occupy considerable areas of Transylvania, and there are numbers of them also in the Banat.

The southern part of the Dobrudja was taken by Rumania from Bulgaria after the second Balkan War (1913). This area is Bulgarian and Turkish in population. The Jewish question, which has had a long history in Rumania, recently flared up again with the growth of a Fascist movement deriving its inspiration largely from Nazi ideas.

Rumania's chief exports (when the state of world trade makes exports possible) are wheat and oil. The principal oilfields lie along the southern slopes of the Transylvanian Alps.

MAP 18

CEDED TO
RUMANIA
AFTER
BALKAN WARS

RUMANIA

°Bucharest

Danube

DOBRUDJA

Varna
BLACK
SEA

Sofia
BULGARIA

TURKEY
Constantinople

□ Territory claimed by
Bulgaria after First
Balkan War, 1912-13

▨ Territory finally gained
after Second Balkan War.
(1913)

▨ Territory outside black frontier
line was lost after Great War.
(1919)

MONTE-
NEGRO

SERBIA

Uskub

MACEDONIA

Salonika°

Dedeagatch

Dardanelles

AEGEAN
SEA

ALBANIA

GREECE

MONTE-
NEGRO

A D R I A T I C

Durazzo

Valona

Miles

0   100   200   300   500

J.F.H.

36

BULGARIA

BULGARIA has been described as "the Hungary of the Balkans." Like Hungary, she wants Treaty revision; and she has double cause for resentment since, as well as in 1918, she remembers 1913, when the fruits of the wars in which Turkey was defeated by the Balkan allies went in the main to her neighbours. In 1912 she was the most powerful of the Balkan states. In 1918 she stood alone, weakest of them all. In 1913 she had to acquiesce in Serbia's acquisition of Macedonia, while Greece occupied Salonika, and Rumania, in the north, took the southern Dobrudja. She did indeed gain a foothold on the coast of the Aegean; but in 1918 this also was lost.

Her foreign policy since the War has been largely dictated by the Macedonian "irredentist" organisation whose dominant idea is a permanent blood-feud with Yugo-Slavia. But it is probable that fear of the *"Drang nach Osten"* aims of a Nazi Germany may encourage a more conciliatory attitude on the part of her neighbours of the Little Entente.

The population of Bulgaria, like Rumania, is mainly peasant; and in both countries repressive measures against a bitterly discontented peasantry have been a feature of political life during the past few years. A somewhat bewildering succession of *coups* by Army officers and counter-*coups* by King Boris have resulted in the promise of a new constitution.

MAP 19

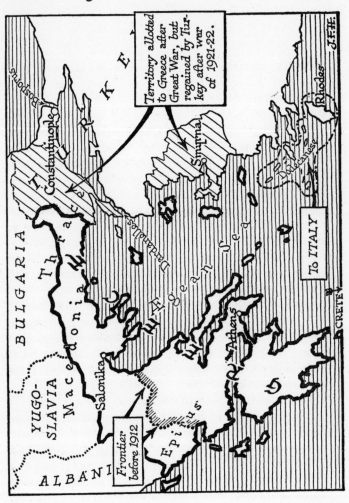

Territory allotted to Greece after Great War, but regained by Turkey after war of 1921-22.

BULGARIA

YUGO-SLAVIA

ALBANIA

Bosporus

Constantinople

T U R K E Y

Smyrna

Rhodes

Dodecanese

TO ITALY

CRETE

Thrace

Macedonia

Salonika

Dardanelles

Aegean Sea

Athens

Epirus

Frontier before 1912

—J.F.H.

GREECE

GREECE—ancient and modern—may be said to consist rather of the coasts and islands of a sea, the Aegean, than a single block of mainland territory. After the Balkan wars against Turkey (1912-13) she extended her hold on that sea by acquiring part of its northern coast-line, including Salonika. Following the Great War the Allies increased her hold again by carrying her territory right up to within a few miles of Constantinople; and established her on the eastern (Asia Minor) coast of the Aegean by giving her Smyrna and its hinterland, as well as several of the islands. Smyrna and Eastern Thrace were lost after her disastrous war with Turkey (1921-22). During recent years Greek governments have established amicable relations with Turkey, beginning with the organised exchange (with League of Nations financial assistance) of their respective nationals from one territory to another, and culminating in an explicit Pact of Friendship (1933), which guaranteed the inviolability of common frontiers and provided for common action on all international questions.

Greek nationalist ambitions are still affronted by the Italian occupation of Rhodes (an important naval base) and the Dodecanese islands; and by Britain's continued hold on Cyprus (*cf.* map 26, "Mediterranean Problems"). The recent unsuccessful revolt in Greece was, according to a statement by M. Venizelos, inspired by the hope of Italian assistance, but this failed to materialise.

MAP 20

MINORITIES IN
EASTERN AND
CENTRAL EUROPE

The War and the Treaties, with the ensuing triumph of various small nationalities—previously minorities—enormously increased the dangers of the minorities problem in Central and Eastern Europe. An ethnographical map of the area shows a tangled patchwork of races and languages. The Treaties themselves, as well as certain special Minorities Treaties concluded by the victorious Allies with Poland, Czechoslovakia, Yugo-Slavia, Rumania and Greece, give League of Nations guarantees to minorities. In addition, certain states have entered into direct engagements with the League to observe similar minority rights. The conditions under which minorities may lodge a complaint with the Council of the League are, however, hedged about with many delays and formalities; and the League has accordingly but seldom intervened to question the "sovereign" rights of any state concerned. A case in point is Polish Ukraine (*cf.* map 7) which has several times unsuccessfully petitioned the League for the autonomy promised it under the original Treaty.

(N.B. (i) The map shows only the principal minorities in each case. (ii) The word "Ukrainian" covers the Ruthenians of Poland and Rumania.)

41

MAP 21

NEW EUROPEAN
STATES

Not even in those parts of the world where frontiers are arbitrarily set up or altered by all-conquering alien imperialisms did the War make greater changes than in Europe itself; where the Treaties of 1919 set up six new independent sovereign states. This was done ostensibly on the principle of nationality, though the "rights" of these smaller peoples, conveniently for the Allies, coincided with the need to break up defeated Powers—and guard against revolutionary ones. It will be noted that four of the six—Finland, Estonia, Latvia and Lithuania—and a large part of the fifth—Poland —were formerly Russian territory; while the sixth— Czechoslovakia—was part of pre-war Austria-Hungary.

The first five have access to the Baltic Sea, though Poland's coast-line was contrived by a territorial arrangement (the "Corridor") which has in it plentiful potentialities of further trouble. The sixth, Czechoslovakia, is a land-locked state whose waterway communication with the outer world must needs be by rivers (*cf.* next map).

MAP 22

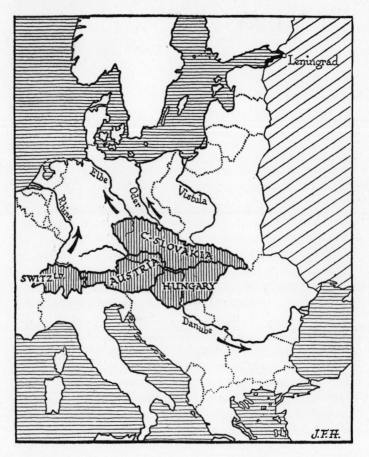

INLAND STATES
OF EUROPE

Before the War there were but two inland states in Europe—Switzerland and Serbia. The Treaties added three more—Austria, Czechoslovakia and Hungary. (And it should be noted that Russia's western coast-line was cut down to the small strip on the Gulf of Finland.)

Waterway communications being essential to a state, certain of the main rivers of Europe took on a new—and international—importance. Chief of these are the Rhine, Elbe and Oder, all largely German rivers; and the Danube, which, though it rises in German terri-tory, is a waterway for the countries lying to the south of Germany. All these rivers are now subject to some measure of international control. Thus Switzerland has been given special rights of navigation on the Rhine, and Czechoslovakia on the Elbe and Oder (Hamburg, at the mouth of the former being Czecho-slovakia's chief northern port of export).

The Danube is under the control of a European Commission consisting—in accordance with the bad old principle of intervention by the great Powers in Balkan affairs—of four national delegates, only one of them from a Danubian country—Rumania; the others representing Britain, France and Italy.

MAP 23

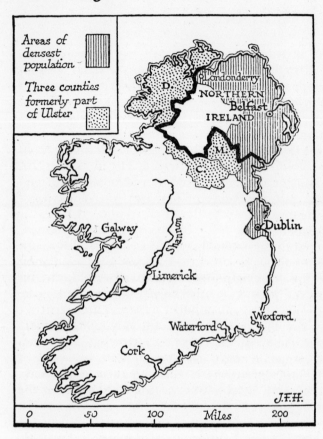

Areas of densest population

Three counties formerly part of Ulster

D.

Londonderry

NORTHERN

Belfast

IRELAND

M.

C.

Galway

Shannon

Limerick

Dublin

Waterford

Wexford

Cork

J.F.H.

0   50   100   Miles   200

IRELAND

THE DIVISION OF IRELAND into two separate areas, the Irish Free State and Northern Ireland, was an attempt to solve a particularly obstinate "minorities problem." The Protestant minority of the north-east corner refused to join in the demand of the Catholic-Nationalist majority for separation from Great Britain. They were accordingly given a Parliament of their own, as well as representation in the British Parliament. The Free State was accorded dominion status, but the right of secession from the Empire was denied to it.

Ireland's economic problems are aggravated by these fierce political nationalisms and anti-nationalisms. In the first place, nearly a third of the total population and the most important industrial area is cut off from the Free State. In the second, the Free State Government's main problem—of providing (particularly now that emigration to America has been virtually stopped) for the needs of a growing population in a preponderantly agricultural state—is rendered still more difficult by a continuance of the historic quarrel with Britain and the consequent loss of the British market for Irish exports. Mr. de Valera's plan is to make Ireland a self-contained and self-sufficient economic unit. To do this he proposes to break up the big farms and cattle-ranches of the centre and south, and hand over half-a-million acres to peasant farmers. "Land hunger" still remains the dominant fact in internal Irish politics.

MAP 24

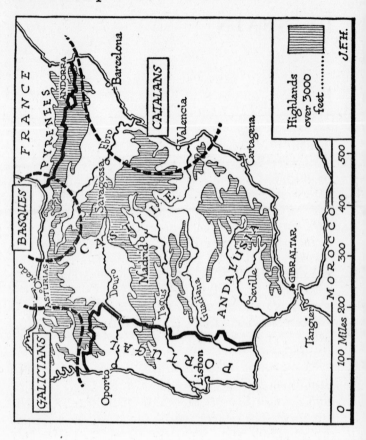

SEPARATIST MOVEMENTS IN SPAIN

EVERYBODY KNOWS that a part of the Iberian peninsula —Portugal—is politically separated from the remainder—Spain. But most of us, at all events until recently, thought that divisions ended there, and that all Spaniards were Spaniards. As a matter of fact, the same geographical factors which made Portugal a separate state from Spain—the division of the peninsula into river valleys with high mountain barriers between— have always operated against unity in Spain itself; and in the political turmoil which preceded and has followed the ending of the Spanish monarchy and the establishment of a republic, various separatist movements have played their part. Galicians in the northwest, Basques in the north, and Catalans on the eastern (Mediterranean) coast all have movements aiming either at complete independence or at some measure of autonomy.

The Spanish crisis of autumn 1934 began with the curtailment by the Government of the powers of provincial councils, especially in the Basque and Catalan provinces. The general strike which followed shifted the emphasis from Separatist to working-class and anti-Fascist demands; and the bloody suppression of the strike in the mining district of Asturias, in which the Government made use of Moorish troops, has resulted in the bitterest feeling throughout the whole of Spain.

MAP 25

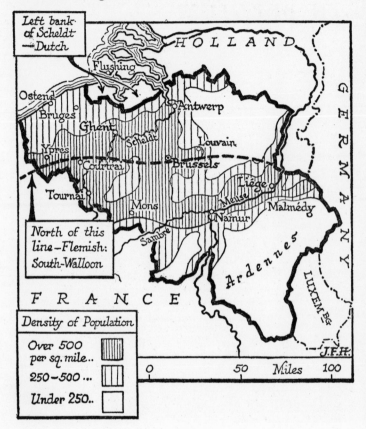

Left bank of Scheldt—Dutch

HOLLAND

Flushing

Ostend
Bruges
Ghent
Ypres
Courtrai
Tournai
Mons
Antwerp
Louvain
Brussels
Scheldt
Liége
Meuse
Namur
Malmédy
Sambre
Ardennes

North of this line—Flemish: South—Walloon

GERMANY

LUXEMBG

FRANCE

J.F.H.

Density of Population

Over 500 per sq. mile..

250—500 ...

Under 250..

0   50   Miles   100

NATIONALITIES
IN BELGIUM

THE QUARREL between the Walloons, or French-speaking Belgians, and the Flemings, whose language is a version of Dutch, was embittered during the War years when some of the Flemish leaders worked with the Germans, then occupying Belgium, to form an independent Flemish state under German protection. This action on the part of a small group led the Walloons afterwards to accuse the Flemings in general of disloyalty to the Belgian state. The dispute was recently revived when the question of the reappointment of government officials who had been dismissed for "unpatriotic conduct" during the War resulted in an acute division within the Belgian Cabinet itself. The Flemings have been successful in securing official recognition for the Flemish tongue, and the University of Ghent has been "Flammandised."

The map also illustrates a problem which was for some time the source of some friction between Holland and Belgium—the control of the left bank of the Scheldt. The present frontier puts the Dutch on both sides of the river estuary, and for the greater security of the port of Antwerp the Belgians demanded that this should be altered (*cf.* map 2).

MAP 26

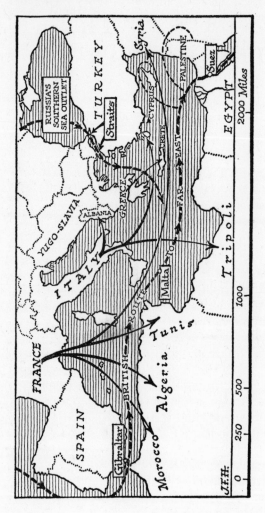

CONFLICTING INTERESTS IN THE MEDITERRANEAN

Since the "opening-up" of Africa by the Powers and in particular since the cutting of the Suez Canal, the Mediterranean has become the centre of various competing national interests. To France, direct communication with her north African empire is vital. Italy, too, has her interests in Tripoli and—*via* Suez—in her colonial possessions on the Red Sea; she, too (as already noted, map 13), seeks undisputed control of the Adriatic. From west to east of the sea runs the British high-road to India, with its key-points at Gibraltar, Malta, Cyprus, and Suez. Greece resents the Italian occupation of Rhodes and the Dodecanese Islands, and the British occupation of Cyprus. Russia is concerned in the "balance of power" in the eastern Mediterranean, since the Straits (Bosporus and Dardanelles) leading from the Black Sea are the sea-outlet to her whole southern coast-line.

MAP 27

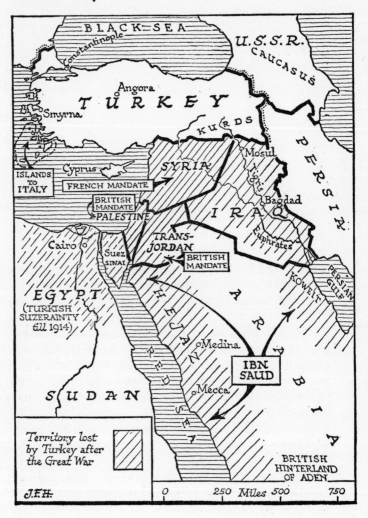

BLACK SEA

Constantinople

U.S.S.R.

CAUCASUS

Angora

TURKEY

Smyrna

KURDS

Mosul

PERSIA

Tigris

Cyprus

SYRIA

ISLANDS
TO
ITALY

FRENCH MANDATE

BRITISH
MANDATE
PALESTINE

Bagdad

IRAQ

Cairo

Suez
SINAI

TRANS-
JORDAN

BRITISH
MANDATE

Euphrates

KOWEIT

PERSIAN
GULF

EGYPT
(TURKISH
SUZERAINTY
till 1914)

A

HEJAN

RED SEA

Medina

R

B

I

A

IBN
SAUD

SUDAN

Mecca

Territory lost
by Turkey after
the Great War

BRITISH
HINTERLAND
OF ADEN

J.F.H.

0   250   Miles   500   750

54

TURKEY'S WAR LOSSES

THE BALKAN WARS (1912-13) resulted in the ending of Turkish overlordship of other races in Europe. The settlement after the Great War ended also her rule over the Arabs of Syria, Mesopotamia and Arabia proper; as well as her suzerainty over Egypt. Turkey's population is now predominantly Turkish, her only minority problem being that of the Kurds who dwell in the mountain country round about the head waters of the Tigris and Euphrates (and who extend also into northern Syria and Iraq).

Syria was made a French mandate; Palestine, Transjordania and Iraq, British (Iraq later attaining independence). The patchwork of Arab kingdoms, emirates and chieftainships set up—or bolstered up—by the Allies further south has been considerably modified by the conquests of Ibn Saud (*cf.* map 33).

MAP 28

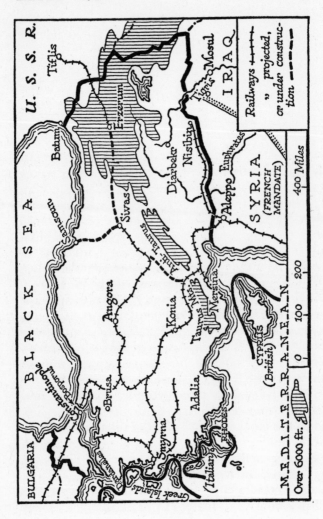

TURKEY

AFTER HAVING FOUGHT four wars in ten years—against Italy (in Tripoli) 1911-12, against the Balkan Allies, 1912, as one of Germany's allies in the Great War, 1914-18, and against Greece, 1921-22—Turkey has since settled down, under the dictatorship of Mustapha Kemal, to peace through a mainly isolationist policy. Confined to Constantinople and its hinterland in Europe and to the vast uplands of the Anatolian Plateau, Kemal has resolutely worked for the internal development of Turkish territory. His plans include large schemes of road and rail development, including a Trans-Anatolian railway connecting the port of Samsoun on the Black Sea with Mersina on the Mediterranean, and another line which would connect Angora with the Russian frontier. (Several of the lines shown in the map as "under construction" are now practically completed.) Ever since the War the new Turkey has enjoyed the friendliest relations with the U.S.S.R. and more recently has made an alliance with its western neighbour—and ex-enemy—Greece (*cf.* map 19, and, for Russian frontier, map 57).

N. B. By Government decree the name of Constantinople has now been changed to Istanbul.

MAP 29

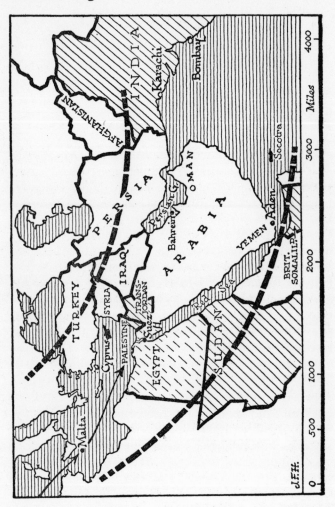

BRITISH INTERESTS
IN THE NEAR EAST

THE WHOLE BELT of territories bordering the eastern Mediterranean and lying between the Red Sea and the Persian Gulf are of vital concern to Britain since they command her most important strategic highway— the short sea-way and air-route to India and the Indian Ocean. It was this sea-route which was threatened by pre-war Germany's plans for a Berlin-Bagdad railway, an overland route running across Turkey to the Persian Gulf. And because of imperial Britain's interest in the inviolability of her main lines of communication, Egyptian independence cannot be absolute and Ibn Saud's approaches to Trans-Jordan must be closely watched. The Turkish hold on this block of territory was, as we have already seen (*cf.* map 27, ended by the Great War.

MAP 30

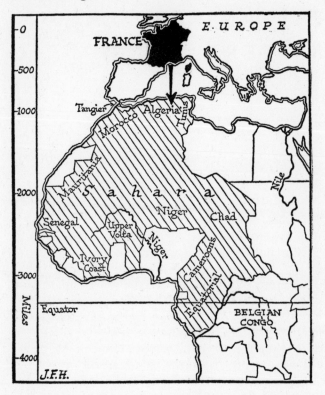

FRANCE AND THE WESTERN MEDITERRANEAN

THOUGH HER SYRIAN MANDATE carries her interests into the eastern Mediterranean, France's main concern is the maintenance of uninterrupted communications, at the western end of that sea, with her African empire. With the completion of her conquest of Morocco (excepting for the small Spanish zone, and the international zone of Tangier) and the addition to her equatorial territories (by mandate) of the Cameroons, previously a German colony, France's African possessions extend from the Mediterranean coast nearly 3,000 miles southward, across the Sahara. And these vast territories are a source, not only of valuable raw materials, but of man-power. Madagascar, off the east coast of Africa, and Indo-China, in the Far East, are also French possessions; but here, in Western and Central Africa, are concentrated France's most important imperial interests, and the Mediterranean sea-link with them is consequently of the first importance to her.

MAP 31

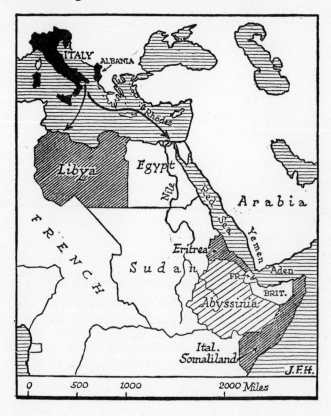

ITALY AND THE
RED SEA

ITALY's three African possessions are Libya (Tripoli), a mainly desert area whose coast faces Italy's own on the further side of the Mediterranean; and Eritrea and Somaliland, on the Red Sea and the Gulf of Aden. The position of the two last gives her a peculiar interest in the development of Abyssinia (see next map). An agreement (1919) between Italy and Britain recognised Italy's interest in the construction of a railway across Abyssinia, linking Eritrea with Somaliland, and in railways carrying Abyssinian products to Italian ports.

Her position in Eritrea also makes Italy interested in the status of the Yemen, the Arabian kingdom on the opposite shore of the Red Sea, whose independence has been threatened by the all-conquering Ibn Saud, ruler of Arabia.

MAP 32

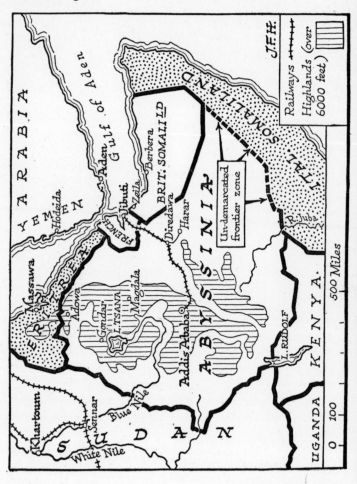

ABYSSINIA

ITALIAN RELATIONS with Abyssinia date from the time, fifty years ago, when Italy occupied Massawa, the nucleus of the colony of Eritrea, and also established a protectorate over a part of what later became the colony of Italian Somaliland. Ten years later, in 1895, an Italian invasion of Abyssinia from the north was utterly defeated by the forces of the Emperor Menelik. The frontier between Abyssinia and Italian Somaliland has never been precisely defined, and it was in this area that the incidents of 1934 took place which have led to the Italian demands for "compensation," and to Abyssinia's appeal to the League of Nations.

British interests in Abyssinia are based on the fact that the head waters of the Blue Nile, vitally important for the irrigation of the Sudan, are in Lake Tsana. Control of the only railway in the country linking Addis Ababa, the capital, with the Gulf of Aden, is in the hands of the French, who hold the port Jibuti and its hinterland. The recent Franco-Italian agreement is stated to have given Italy an interest in the line.

MAP 33

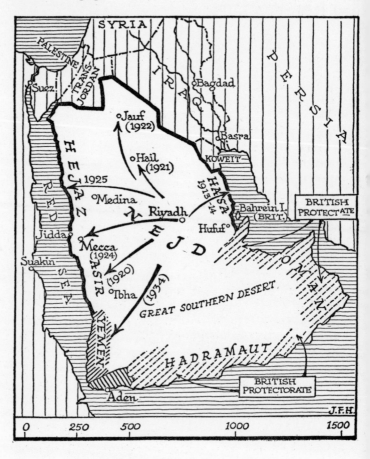

THE CONQUESTS OF
IBN SAUD

THE DISPOSITION of Arab territories after the Great War established in the north, as we have noted (*cf.* map 27), mandates divided between Britain and France. In Arabia proper the kingdom of the Hejaz (on the Red Sea coast) was to receive special British protection, and its ruler claimed overlordship of the rest of the peninsula. This arrangement was shattered by the rise to power of Ibn Saud, leader of the Wahabi sect of the Moslems and ruler of Nejd, in the interior. Before the War Ibn Saud had already conquered Hasa, on the Persian Gulf, from the Turks. After the War he rapidly extended his power by taking the chieftain-ships of Hail and Jauf, to the north, and actually raiding Trans-Jordan; and Asir, on the Red Sea, south of the Hejaz. In 1924-25 he conquered the Hejaz itself, thus consolidating his power from west to east of Arabia. The Yemen, north of Aden on the Red Sea, was attacked in April–May, 1934. The Sultanates of Oman and the Hadramaut, to the south and south-east, as yet remain independent of his rule.

In 1927 a treaty was signed at Jidda between Britain and Ibn Saud, by which the former recognised the complete independence of Ibn Saud's dominions. The name of the latter was in 1932 changed from the "Kingdom of the Hejaz and Nejd" to the "Kingdom of Saudi Arabia."

MAP 34

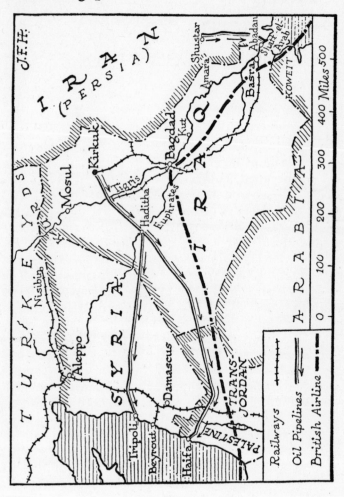

IRAQ:
OIL AND
COMMUNICATIONS

Two factors have given peculiar importance to the new state of Iraq, created by the post-war settlement which ended Turkish rule over the Arabs: oil and British imperial communications. The Kirkuk oilfield, in the vilayet of Mosul, has proved to be of first-rate importance. France fought hard for the inclusion of the Mosul area in her Syrian mandate, and has succeeded in her claim to a proportion of the oil produced, so that the great trans-desert pipeline now completed has a branch leading to the port of Tripoli, in Syria. The British section links Kirkuk with Haifa, in Palestine.

The main British air-route to India and the east passes through Bagdad. Now, indeed, that the aeroplane has become a vital factor in imperial communications, the old land routes between the Mediterranean and the Indian Ocean, via Bagdad, have regained the importance they possessed before the discovery of the Cape route to the Indies.

The British mandate over Iraq ended in 1932, when Iraq became a full member of the League of Nations; but British air bases are still maintained in Iraq, and the Royal Air Force is a factor of considerable importance in the internal affairs of the country.

MAP 35

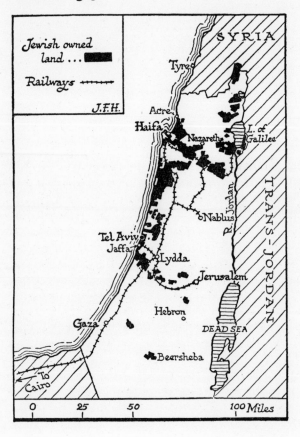

Jewish owned land ...

Railways ┈┈┈┈

J.F.H.

SYRIA

Tyre

Acre
Haifa
Nazareth
L. of Galilee

R. Jordan

TRANS-JORDAN

Nablus

Tel Aviv
Jaffa
Lydda
Jerusalem

Hebron

DEAD SEA

Gaza

Beersheba

To Cairo

0   25   50   100 Miles

JEWISH SETTLEMENTS IN PALESTINE

British declarations during the Great War, on the one hand to the Jews—guaranteeing the establishment of a Jewish national home in Palestine—and on the other to the Arabs—promising the independence of all Arab territories—were difficult to reconcile; as the Mandatory Power in Palestine has since on several occasions discovered. The present population of Palestine is a little over a million, of whom 73 per cent are Moslems and 17 per cent Jews; this latter figure being rather more than double what it was before the British mandatory government was established. About one-third of the Jewish population is settled on the land. The Zionist Organisation, which under the Mandate is recognised as the official Jewish Agency for Palestine, directly montrols many of these settlements, which are situated in the main along the coast between Jaffa and Acre, in the Esdraelon valley (south of Haifa-Nazareth), and near the Sea of Galilee. The main problem of the administration is, of course, that of absorbing new Jewish immigrants without adversely affecting the existing Arab population.

(For Haifa, *cf.* map 34.)

MAP 36

U. · S. · S. · R.

Mery

AFGHANISTAN

Tabriz

Kirkuk

Asterabad

Teheran

Kasr-i-Sirin

PROJECTED

Bagdad

I R A Q

Shustar

Yezd

Duzdab

Basra

BALUCHISTAN (INDIA)

Koweit

Bushire

Bandar Abbas

Bahrein Is.

Persian Gulf

Oil wells ●
Original limit of
Anglo-Persian Co.'s
concessions ⚏⚏⚏
Railways +─+─+─

0   250   Miles   500   750

J.F.H.

PERSIA¹—OIL AND
RAILWAYS

Before the Great War the independent sovereign state of Persia was divided into Russian (northern) and British (southern) spheres of influence. But even earlier certain British interests had secured extensive rights over the greater part of the country. The D'Arcy concession (1901), which was the beginning of the Anglo-Persian Oil Company's operations, gave exclusive rights to prospect for oil up to a line (shown in the map) running north-west and south-east from Tehran.

In 1932 the Persian Government cancelled the concession; which event was something of an international incident, since the British Government is a shareholder in the Anglo-Persian Co. A new agreement (June, 1933) revised the financial terms of the concession, and cut down the territory to be exploited by about half (the exact delimitation to be agreed upon later). Under the vigorous regime of Riza Shah Pahlevi, Persia has also objected to the British protectorate over the Bahrein Islands in the Persian Gulf.

Persia is almost a rail-less country. Lines from Russia (Caucasus), Iraq and Baluchistan cross the frontiers to Tabriz, Kasr-i-Sirin and Duzdad respectively. A railway running northwards from the Persian Gulf, alongside the oil pipeline, is to be continued to the Caspian Sea.

¹ Now, by official decree, to be styled Iran.

MAP 37

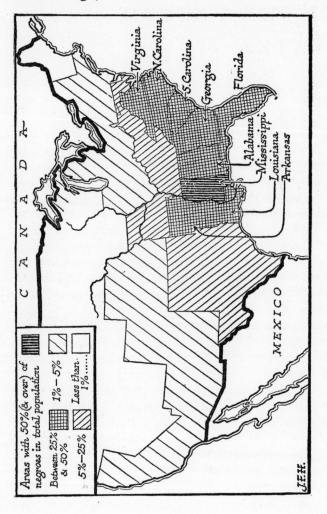

Areas with 50% (& over) of negroes in total population.

Between 25% & 50%

5%–25%

1%–5%

Less than 1%..........

Virginia. N.Carolina. S.Carolina. Georgia. Florida. Alabama. Mississippi. Louisiana. Arkansas.

CANADA

MEXICO

J.F.H.

THE NEGRO PROBLEM
IN THE UNITED
STATES

THE UNITED STATES has a minorities problem of its
own to face, and it can hardly be said at the moment
that the problem is growing easier. There are close
on 12 million negroes in the United States, rather more
than 10 per cent of the total population. The greatest
concentration is, of course, in the southern states of
the cotton belt. In only one state, Mississippi, are the
negroes now in an absolute majority, but in several
others they constitute not much less than half of the
population. In South Carolina, for example, which
in 1920 had 55 per cent negro population, the figure
had fallen to just under 50 per cent in 1930; and there
are areas in all the southern states, including Texas,
where the negroes form a majority. The 1930 census
figures show a small decline in the rural negro population of these states, a decrease doubtless due to the
northward migration of negroes which began during
the War.

Racial feeling in the U.S., despite some signs to
the contrary, cannot be said to be growing less bitter.
It is, indeed, somewhat difficult to distinguish between
the anti-Semitism of Hitler's Germany and the negro-
phobia of a great part of the United States.

MAP 38

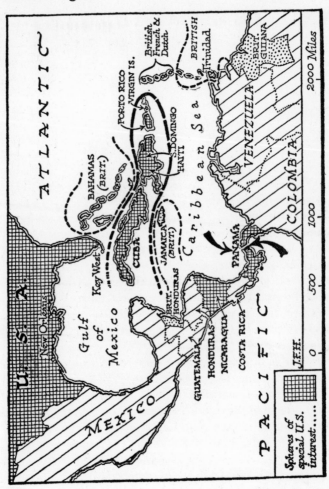

THE UNITED STATES
AND THE CARIBBEAN

FROM THE TIME of the war with Spain (1898) United States penetration in the Caribbean area—the islands of the West Indies and the smaller states of Central America—steadily proceeded. After the Spanish War the island of Porto Rico was annexed, and Cuba became virtually an American protectorate. The new republic of Panama was brought under "general supervision" in 1903, the United States obtaining permanent rights in the Canal Zone. Intervention in Haiti in 1915 led to a supervision of Haitian finances; and in the neighbouring negro republic of Santo Domingo a receivership, amounting to a protectorate, was instituted. In 1916 Nicaragua became a virtual protectorate, granting exclusive rights in a hypothetical canal to the United States. In 1917 certain of the Virgin Islands were purchased from Denmark.

The special United States sphere in the islands is flanked north and south (*cf.* map) by British possessions—the Bahamas and Jamaica.

MAP 39

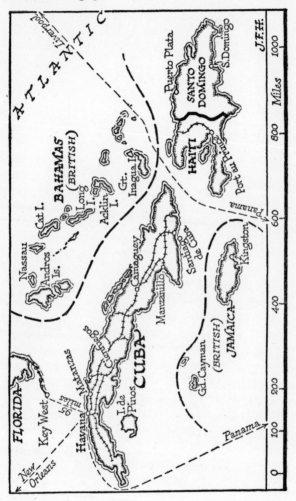

CUBA

By the Platt Amendment (abrogated May, 1934) the United States established a protectorate over the island of Cuba after the Spanish-American War. The recent Cuban revolution was in part a nationalist rising against United States domination; but Cuba's fundamental grievances are economic. The island's staple product is sugar, and it has been the rigid limitation of its exports to the United States, in the interests of the American sugar beet industry, which has destroyed the foundations of Cuba's economic life.

MAP 40

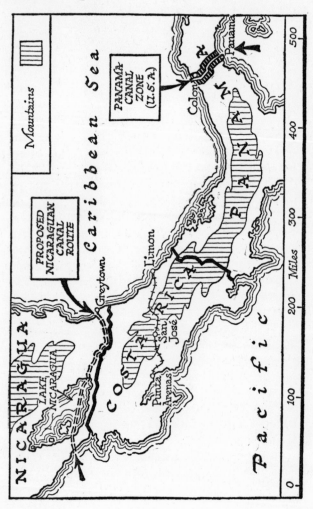

PANAMA AND
NICARAGUA

THE SPANISH-AMERICAN WAR had made clear the urgent necessity of an inter-oceanic canal through the central American peninsula unless the United States was to keep a battle fleet in both the Pacific and Atlantic Oceans. Panama, formerly a province of the republic of Colombia, declared its independence on November 3rd, 1903. It was recognised ten days later by the United States Government, which five days later signed a Treaty with the new republic providing facilities for the construction of the Panama Canal. The Canal Zone, which extends five miles on each side of the canal, was granted in perpetuity to the United States.

In 1916, the Panama Canal having already proved inadequate for the sea traffic which used it, the United States Government signed a Treaty with Nicaragua giving it the option for a canal route (*cf.* map), and a naval base on both the Atlantic and Pacific coasts. No work has ever been started on the scheme, as it was estimated that the total cost would be 700 million dollars, and that a third set of locks on the Panama Canal could be constructed for a fifth of that sum. American marines, who had been in occupation for a considerable period, evacuated Nicaragua in January 1933.

MAP 41

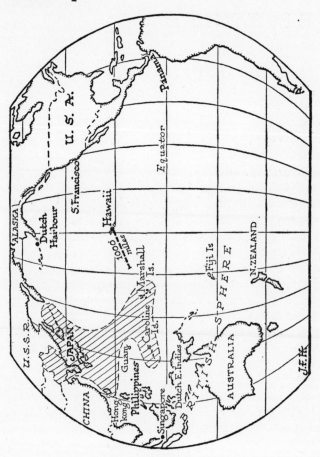

RIVAL INTERESTS IN
THE PACIFIC

Hawaii, the half-way house of the Pacific, was annexed by the United States in 1898. A few months later the Philippine Islands and Guam Island were taken over and the United States had become a Pacific Power. After the Great War, the German Pacific islands north of the Equator (*cf*. map 48) were handed over as mandates to Japan. This brought the Japanese sphere directly across the main lines of communication between Panama and the Pacific ports of the United States and her far eastern possessions. Naval experts have opined that the U.S. Navy could not operate effectively more than 1000 miles away from Hawaii.

The measure of Philippine independence granted by the U.S. involves some American control until 1945–6. Whether American withdrawal will not sooner or later mean Japanese intervention seems scarcely doubtful. Japanese dominance in this area would presumably be regarded by Britain with some apprehension, since it would bring a powerful rival much closer to Hong-Kong, Singapore and the oil of the Dutch East Indies.

MAP 42

Eastern Industrial Areas of the U.S.

U. S.

New York

Panama

Callao

Antofagasta

Valparaiso

Buenos Aires

ARGENTINE

C. Horn

PACIFIC

ATLANTIC

BRITISH ISLES same scale

J.F.H.

"YANQUI IMPERIALISMO" IN LATIN AMERICA

U NITED STATES penetration in the Caribbean area has been watched with considerable suspicion by the Latin American Republics. The Panama Canal has, moreover, brought the states of the Pacific coast thousands of miles nearer to the eastern industrial area of the United States; and the U.S. has intended to re-interpret the Monroe Doctrine as giving to itself exclusive rights of intervention in South America.

Latin America is a main battleground of British and American commercial and financial interests. The battle is fiercest in the Argentine, commercially the most developed of the South American countries. A British Treaty with the Argentine (1933) gave various commercial advantages to Britain; but over the whole of the continent between 1913 and 1927 Britain's share of the total South American imports dropped from 25 per cent to 16 per cent, while that of the United States rose from 24 per cent to 38 per cent.

MAP 43

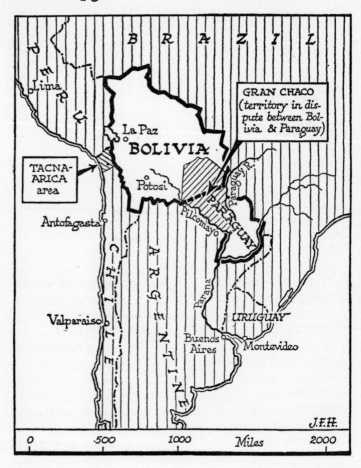

- P E R U
- Lima
- B R A Z I L
- La Paz
- **BOLIVIA**
- Potosi
- GRAN CHACO
(*territory in dis-*
pute between Bol-
ivia & Paraguay)
- TACNA-
ARICA
area
- Antofagasta
- Pilcomayo
- Paraguay R.
- PARAGUAY
- C H I L E
- A R G E N T I N E
- Parana
- Valparaiso
- URUGUAY
- Buenos
Aires
- Montevideo

J.F.H.

| 0 | 500 | 1000 | Miles | 2000 |

THE BOLIVIA-PARAGUAY WAR

WAR BETWEEN the two inland states of South America—Bolivia and Paraguay—has been going on for some time. The area in dispute is the Gran Chaco territory. Bolivia, cut off by the Andes from easy access to the Pacific, desires direct water communication down the Paraguay and Parana rivers to the Atlantic seaboard. Paraguay, on the other hand, claims a considerable area of Bolivian territory. Moreover, oil has been discovered in the Chaco; which makes its possession of some importance.

At one time Bolivia laid claim to the Tacna-Arica area (see map), which would have given her direct communication with the Pacific coast; but by the agreement of 1929 this area was divided between Peru and Chile.

MAP 44

BOLIVIA

Of ALL the countries of the New World, Bolivia ranks second only to the United States and Mexico in mineral wealth. She produces a quarter of the tin output of the world. Next to China she is the world's chief source of antimony. Silver and lead are also mined. Her exports must go across Chilean territory to the Pacific ports of Arica and Antofagasta. Her other possible outlet, *via* the Paraguay river to the Atlantic, is the present cause of her war with Paraguay. The majority of Bolivia's population is native Indian. A recent writer has remarked that "a raw material of great importance to modern industry and a primitive, poverty-stricken and inarticulate native population are the two basic facts of Bolivian economic life."

MAP 45

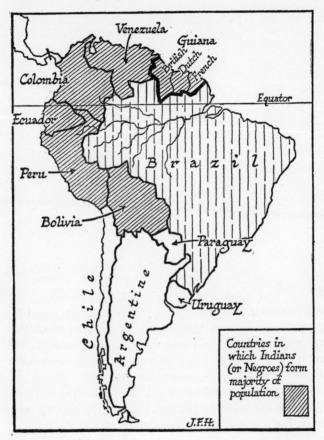

Countries in which Indians (or Negroes) form majority of population

NATIONALITIES IN
SOUTH AMERICA

EUROPEANS usually think of South America as including only one colonial area, that of Guiana, divided
between British, Dutch and French; but in four of
the South American republics—Colombia, Ecuador,
Peru and Bolivia—the native Indians form a majority
of the population and, these all being mining countries, a source of degradingly cheap labour power. In
Venezuela and Guiana negroes and mulattos constitute a majority. In Brazil the proportion of white and
Indian inhabitants is about equal and there is also a
very considerable mulatto population. Only in the
four republics of the temperate zone in the south are
the native races in a relatively small minority.

MAP 46

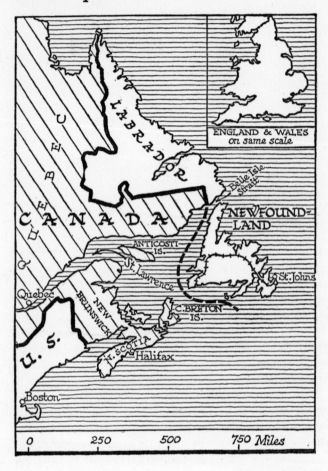

ENGLAND & WALES
on same scale

LABRADOR

QUEBEC

CANADA

Belle Isle Strait

NEWFOUND-
LAND

ANTICOSTI
IS.

St. Lawrence

Quebec

NEW BRUNSWICK

St. Johns

C. BRETON
IS.

U. S.

N. SCOTIA

Halifax

Boston

| 0 | 250 | 500 | 750 Miles |

92

NEWFOUNDLAND

THE REPORT of a Royal Commission (November, 1933) recommended that the dominion of Newfoundland should lose its representative institutions for an indefinite period of years, its administraton to be taken over by a Commission appointed by the British Government. This course was necessitated by the bankruptcy of the Newfoundland Government, and the British Treasury had to take over in order to avoid Newfoundland default on debt payments.

The principal industry of the island, which has a population of a quarter of a million, is fishing, and there are considerable timber resources. The Labrador coast has always been administered by the Newfoundland Government. The actual boundary between Labrador and the province of Quebec, in Canada, was fixed by the Privy Council in 1927. The population of Labrador in 1931 was 4,264.

MAP 47

THE POWERS IN THE FAR EAST

THE FAR EASTERN PROBLEM is the problem of China. That vast country, with its hard-working millions of peasant farmers, would in all probability have lost its independence as and when India did but for its greater distance from Europe. It was the coming of the steamship which brought China "within range," and began the process of her dissolution. For the main ways into China were sea ways, a great mountain barrier cutting her off from the rest of Asia on the west, and Russia controlling the land approaches from the north. During the latter half of the 19th century and the earlier years of the 20th, the great colonial Powers steadily encroached upon her borders and established themselves, for purposes of trade, in "treaty ports" within her actual territory.

The map shows the grouping of the four main Powers: Japan—the "Power on the spot"—established on the mainland in Korea and Manchukuo; the United States in the Philippines;[1] Britain at Hong-Kong, commanding the southern (Canton) gateway into China, and at Singapore, nearly 1,500 miles to the south; France in Indo-China. Russia, which in Czarist days had a special sphere of interest in Manchuria, is now cut off from direct contact with China by the Japanese occupation of that country.

[1] The position here is somewhat modified by the grant of independence (economic reasons) to the Philippines; but the U. S. retains control of foreign policy, and will presumably continue to regard the islands as an American sphere.

MAP 48

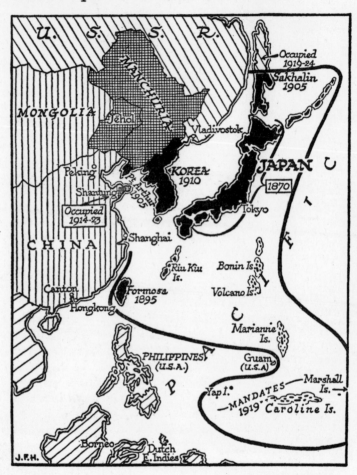

THE EMPIRE OF JAPAN

At the time when the great non-Asiatic Powers began to intervene in Far Eastern affairs the island empire of Japan was still a mediæval feudal state. Within a generation she had remodelled her social system on European capitalist lines and equipped herself with the armaments which were the obvious hall-mark of western civilisation.

The map illustrates her steady growth since she first took part in the race for "expansion." The island of Formosa was acquired after her war with China, 1894–95; Port Arthur and the southern half of Sakhalin Island after the Russo-Japanese war, 1904–5. Korea, whose independence she had professed to secure by the Chinese war, was annexed in 1910.[1] Japan was now established on the mainland. And in the meantime she had been consolidating her position and "rights" in southern Manchuria.

After the Great War she was given the mandate for the ex-German Pacific islands north of the equator; the strategic importance of which is due to their position athwart the direct sea-route from the United States to the Philippines.

Her more recent expansion in Manchuria (now Manchukuo) is dealt with in succeeding maps.

[1] It is worth noting that the present status of Manchukuo, an "independent" state guaranteed by Japan—is precisely similar to that of Korea from 1895 to 1910.

MAP 49

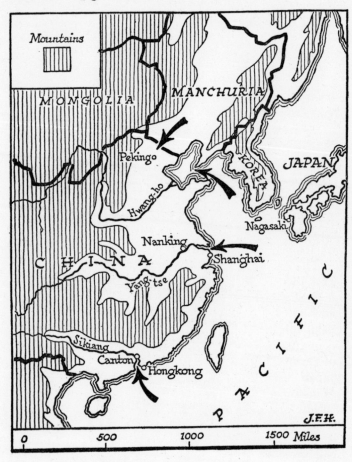

THE WAYS INTO
CHINA

CHINA'S MOST IMPORTANT LINES of communication
are her three great rivers: the Hwang-ho, or Yellow
River in the north; the Yang-tse in the centre; and
the Si-kiang in the south. The mouths of these rivers,
commanding the main routes inland, are accordingly
of first-rate strategic importance.

The southern entry is controlled by the British, at
Hong-Kong. Shanghai, at the mouth of the Yang-tse,
is held jointly by all the alien Powers, with Britain
and America predominating; the Yang-tse itself,
navigable by gunboats for hundreds of miles inland,
is in effect a foreign wedge driven into the very heart
of China. The sea-way in the north is controlled by
Japan, established first in Korea and now also in
Manchuria.

The one practicable land route into China is that
from the north; the route by which the Manchus
entered the country three centuries ago, and for control of which Czarist Russia and Japan struggled in
the years preceding the Great War. It is in this area
that Japan has accomplished the most recent invasion
of China.

MAP 50

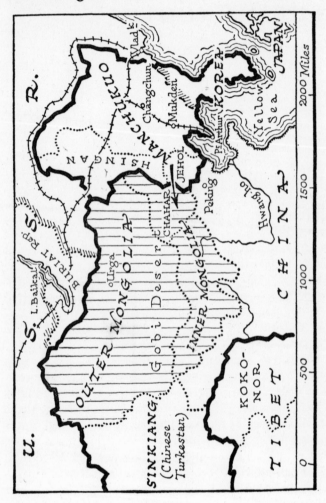

THE LANDS OF
THE MONGOLS

Ever since the Russo-Japanese War (1904-5) Japan
has worked steadily to consolidate her position on the
mainland, and to establish a barrier between Russian
and Chinese territory. By the setting up of the "independent" state of Manchukuo in what was the northern Chinese province of Manchuria, Japan attained
virtual control over enormous economic resources, as
well as providing herself with a safe mainland base for
further aggression, north, east, or south.

Japanese agents and troops have been active more
recently in Inner Mongolia (to the east of Manchukuo). She already rules over some two million Mongols
in the Hsingan province of Manchukuo. Of the three
million other Mongols, about a million live in Outer
Mongolia—a territory half as large as the United States,
but mostly desert; another million in Inner Mongolia;
while about a million are scattered in Chinese Turkestan, in the Kokonor province of Tibet, and in the
Buriat Republic of Asiatic Russia.

MAP 51

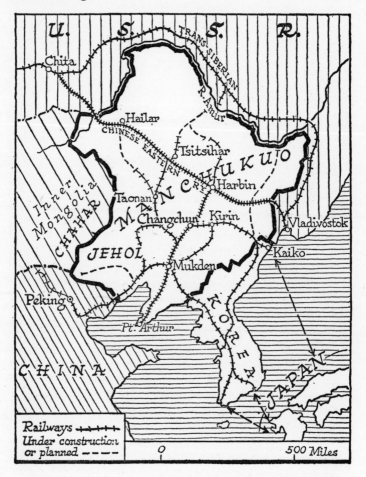

JAPAN AND RUSSIA

THE JAPANESE HOLD on Manchuria is a serious threat to Russia's communications with Eastern Siberia and its Pacific outlet, Vladivostok (see also map 60). The Trans-Siberian railway runs north of the Amur river. In 1896 Czarist Russia made an agreement with China by which a shorter rail route to Vladivostok was to run across northern Manchuria. This was the famous Chinese Eastern Railway. After the Revolution the Soviet government renounced all Russia's privileges in Manchuria, but retained its special rights over this line, and a long series of "incidents" and diplomatic negotiations with Japan followed. Finally, the U.S.S.R. has sold its rights in the railway to the new state of Manchukuo.

The map also shows the network of railways in Manchukuo which have been added by the Japanese to the two original trunk lines—the Chinese Eastern, and the South Manchurian (Port Arthur-Mukden-Changchun).

MAP 52

Areas controlled by Communists or Peasant Soviets

JAPANESE

KOREA

KANSU

SHANSI

SHENSI

CHIHLI (HOPEI)

Peking

Hwangho

SHANTUNG

Kiaochow

HONAN

KIANGSU

ANHWEI

Nanking

Shanghai

SZECHWAN

HUPEH

Yang-tse

Hankow

Kukiang

CHEKIANG

Changsha

HUNAN

KIANGSI

KWEICHOW

FUKIEN

Foochow

YUNNAN

KWANGSI

KWANGTUNG

Sikiang

Canton

Amoy

FORMOSA (Japanese)

Hongkong

FRENCH INDO-CHINA

J.F.H.

0   500   1000   1500 Miles

SOVIET AREAS IN CHINA

THERE IS NOW no unified control over all China. The Nanking Government (*cf.* next map), which is recognised by the Powers as the government of China, is actually only in effective control over the coastal provinces from Shantung down to Fukien, and the lower Yang-tse valley. Peking, nominally subject to Nanking, now appears to be in the hands of a council which is a tool of Japan. The South-Western Council at Canton, heir of Dr. Sun Yat Sen's original National Government, exercises influence in the provinces of Kwang-si and Kwang-tung. Since the split between Lefts and Rights in the Kuomintang, Canton has become the more or less independent headquarters of the Left section.

Inland, north and south of the Middle Yang-tse, are large areas controlled by Soviets of peasants and workers (usually described as "bandits" by their opponents). A Soviet Republic at one time recently covered a great part of the provinces of Kiangsi and Fukien. The Nanking Government has been engaged in armed operations against this area for some years, and recent information—though this is always extremely vague and inadequate—declares that the main Red forces have now been shifted westward, to the province of Szechwan.

MAP 53

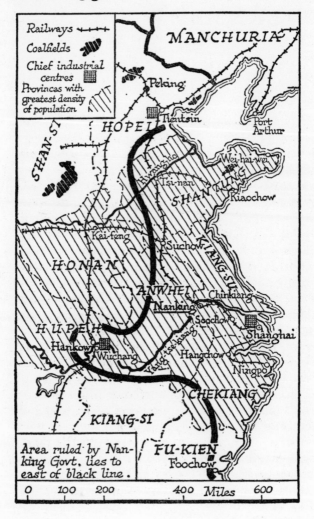

Railways
Coalfields
Chief industrial centres
Provinces with greatest density of population

MANCHURIA

Peking
Tientsin
Port Arthur
HOPEI
Wei-hai-wei
Hwang-ho
Tsi-nan
SHANTUNG
Kiaochow
SHAN-SI
Kai-feng
Suchow
KIANG-SU
HONAN
ANWHEI
Chinkiang
Nanking
Soochow
Shanghai
HUPEH
Hankow
Wuchang
Yang-tsi-kiang
Hangchow
Ningpo
CHEKIANG
KIANG-SI
Area ruled by Nanking Govt. lies to east of black line.
FU-KIEN
Foochow

0   100   200   400   Miles   600

THE NANKING
GOVERNMENT

THE NANKING GOVERNMENT, under Chiang Kai-shek exercises effective control only over the northern and central coastal areas of China: the provinces of Shan-tung, Kiang-su, Chekiang, and parts of An-whei, Hupeh and Fukien. These include the greater portion of the most densely populated regions; as well as the great industrial centres of Shanghai and Han-kow. Such a territory may well become the nucleus of a really homogeneous state. China as a whole is as large as Europe without Russia; and it is probable that, from this area as a base, the unification of the entire country may gradually be carried out. On the other hand, this same area, or at any rate the northern part of it, may become, unless action from other outside Powers prevents it, a protectorate of Japan. Utterances by Japanese statesmen and militarists have asserted Japan's right to "stabilise" the whole of Eastern Asia (i.e., China—and probably Siberia) as she has already "stabilised" Manchuria. And the policy of the Nanking Government seems, particularly since the failure of the League of Nations to come to China's assistance, to be based on acceptance of Japanese dominance.

MAP 54

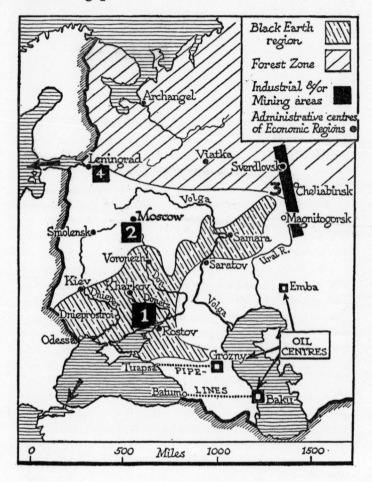

THE NEW RUSSIA

A WORLD FACTOR of the first importance to-day is the new industrialised Russia which the Soviet Government has set itself to build up. Pre-war Russia was predominantly a land of peasants. Technically the country was a century behind the rest of Europe. The revolutionary government set itself from the outset to alter this, and the Five-Year Plan was the first instance in world history of a scheme on a colossal scale for the unified organisation and development of the entire resources of a nation.

The map gives in simplified form the main economic facts of European Russia. The four chief industrial regions are (1) the Ukraine,[1] based on the Donetz coalfield and the iron of Krivoi Rog, and containing the great electric power station of Dnieprostroi; (2) the central (Moscow) area, with mining and manufactures; (3) the Ural region, the minerals of which are being developed in conjunction with the Kusnetz coalfield in western Siberia (cf. map 58); and (4) the Leningrad manufacturing area. The black earth region is, of course, the richest agricultural area. The oilfields of the Caucasus are also shown.

European Russia is divided into twelve economic regions, the administrative centres of which are marked.

[1] See also map 8.

MAP 55

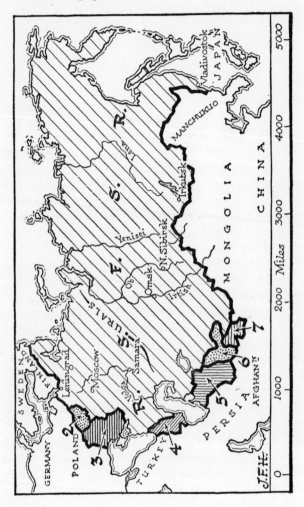

POLITICAL DIVISIONS
OF THE NEW RUSSIA

THE NEW RUSSIA is not only interesting economically. As a federation of partly autonomous states it is a political experiment on a gigantic scale. The Soviet government has had to solve a minorities problem of extraordinary complexity. The 1926 census lists 174 different races who are citizens of the U.S.S.R. The total population is now estimated at between 160 and 170 million, more than three-quarters of whom live in the European area.

The Union consists of seven main Federated Republics, which include many smaller republics and autonomous districts. These are (1) the R.S.F.S.R. (Russian Soviet Federated Socialist Republics), including most of the European area and nearly all Siberia; (2) the White Russian Republic (on the western European frontier); (3) the Ukrainian Republic; (4) the Transcaucasian Federated Republics; (5) Tajikistan; (6) Uzbekistan, and (7) Turkmenistan—these last three in Asia.

MAP 56

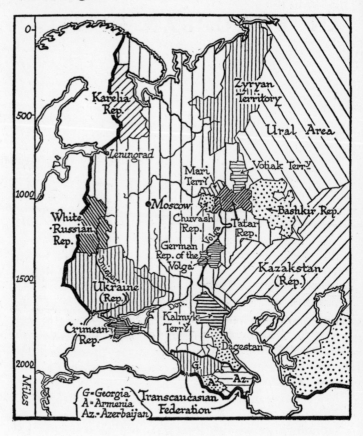

POLITICAL DIVISIONS
OF EUROPEAN RUSSIA

THREE OF THE MAIN Federated Republics of the
U.S.S.R. lie along the western and south-western bor-
ders of European Russia: the White Russian Repub-
lic, the Ukrainian Republic, and the Transcaucasian
Federation of Republics, (Georgia, Armenia and
Azerbaijan).

The remainder of Russian European territory
forms part of the R.S.F.S.R. (see previous map). It
includes autonomous republics like the Crimea, the
Karelian Republic and the German Republic of the
Volga. Some of these republics contain smaller autonomous areas, the whole organisation of the Soviet state
aiming at a maximum of cultural independence com-
bined with rigid unification of economic organisation.

MAP 57

N. CAUCASUS
Astrakhan
Mouth of the Volga
Autonomous Div^{ns}
Maikop
CHERKESS
KARACHAEV
KABARDINO
BALKARIA
OSSETIA
INGUSETIA
CHECHNIA
DAGESTAN
Tuapse
CASPIAN
ABKHASIA (Rep.)
BLACK SEA.
Poti
GEORGIA
Bahum
ADJAR
Tiflis
AZERBAIJAN
Baku
Kars
ARMENIA
Erzerum
NAKHICHEVAN
TURKEY
PERSIA
J.F.H.

| 0 | 100 | 200 | 300 | Miles | 500 | 600 |

THE CAUCASUS

THE CAUCASUS AREA, between the Black Sea and the Caspian, is of enormous economic importance to Russia by reason of its oilfields. The civil war which followed the 1917 revolution lasted in this area until 1921. Thenceforward the Soviet Government set itself to meet the complicated nationalist demands of its inhabitants by an elaborate patchwork of autonomous republics and districts.

The political divisions are: (1) the Northern Caucasus, a "region" of the R.S.F.S.R., with a number of small autonomous divisions (*cf.* map) on its southern border; (2) the autonomous republic of Dagestan, on the Caspian coast; and (3) the Transcaucasian Federation, consisting of the republics of Georgia (capital, Tiflis), Armenia (capital, Erivan) and Azerbaijan (capital, Baku). Each of these three again includes one or two autonomous regions.

MAP 58

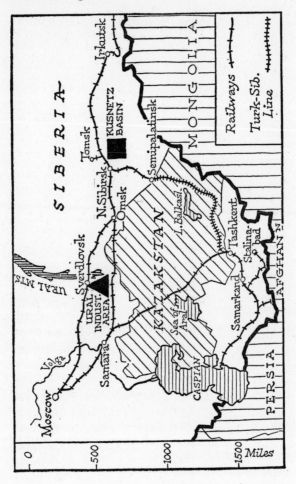

MOScow · Volga · Samara · URAL INDUST. AREA · Sverdlovsk · URAL MTS. · N.Sibirsk · Omsk · Tomsk · KUSNETZ BASIN · Irkutsk · SIBERIA · Semipalatinsk · MONGOLIA · KAZAKSTAN · L. Balkash · Tashkent · Stalina-bad · Samarkand · Sea of Aral · CASPIAN · PERSIA · AFGHAN·N

Railways ————
Turk-Sib. Line ┼┼┼┼┼

0 · 500 · 1000 · 1500 Miles

WESTERN SIBERIA
AND TURKESTAN

ONE OF THE BIG FEATURES of Russia's economic plan is the development of western Siberia and its linking with the European industrial regions. The Kusnetz coal basin, though its working has as yet barely begun, is estimated to contain some 450 billion tons—six times as much as the Donetz field in the Ukraine. It is to be closely linked with the Ural mineral and industrial area.

South of this area is Turkestan, now sub-divided into Kazakstan and various smaller republics (*cf.* next map). This region has been connected with Siberia by the Turk-Sib railway, which follows the old caravan route from Tashkent northwards. It is the longest line constructed in the world during recent years.

MAP 59

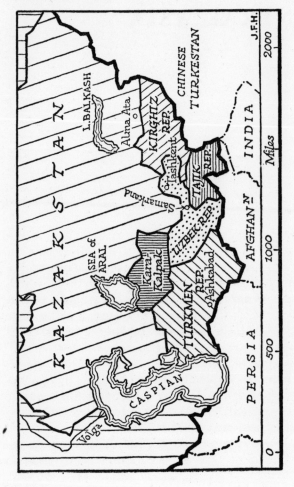

NATIONALITIES IN
CENTRAL ASIA

Turkestan was added to the Russian Empire in the second half of the 19th century. It was this expansion of the Czarist power, touching Afghanistan and approaching the north-western frontier of India, which made the "Russian Bear" the bogey of all good British patriots towards the end of the century. Civil warfare after the revolution did not end in this region until 1924.

The political divisions are now: The Kazakstan republic, largely peopled by nomad Kirghiz; the autonomous region of the Kara-Kalpaks; and the republic of Turkmenistan, inhabited by Mohammedan Turkomans; Uzbekistan, a cotton-producing area with the largest population of the area and the three most important cities of Central Asia—Tashkent, Samarkand and Bokhara; Tajikistan, a mountainous region—in its eastern part are the Pamirs, the "roof of the world"; and Kirghizia, a land of cattle-breeders.

MAP 60

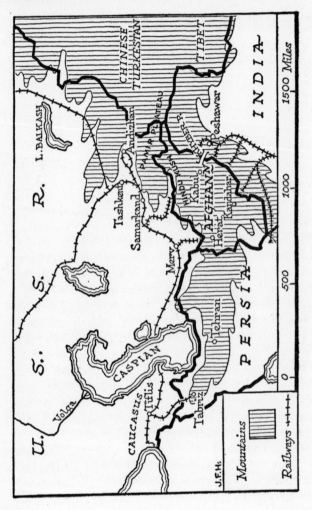

Mountains

Railways

1500 Miles

1000

500

0

J.F.H.

U. S. S. R.

L. BALKASH

CHINESE TURKESTAN

TIBET

INDIA

Volga

CASPIAN

CAUCASUS

Tiflis

Tabriz

Tehran

PERSIA

Marv

Samarkand

Tashkent

Andizhan

PAMIR PLATEAU

HINDU KUSH

Kabul

AFGHANISTAN

Herat

Kandahar

KHYBER P.

Peshawar

CENTRAL ASIAN FRONTIERS AND AFGHANISTAN

AFGHANISTAN is the mountain country separating Asiatic Russia from northern India. Though, as the map shows, it is a country without railways, railway lines lead up to its frontiers north and south. On the Russian side the Central Asian railway has two branches running southward, from Merv and from a point west of Samarkand. On the Indian side the strategic railways of the N.W. Frontier and Baluchistan everywhere stop short of Afghanistan. Schemes for linking the two systems by lines running across Afghanistan, one through Herat and Kandahar, and the second through Kabul to Peshawar, have so far broken down through Russian-British jealousy.

Present British relations with Afghanistan are summarised in a treaty (1921) which recognised the full sovereignty of Afghanistan, with certain British restrictions on special privileges to Russia, and provided for the passage of arms and munitions to Afghanistan through India.

MAP 61

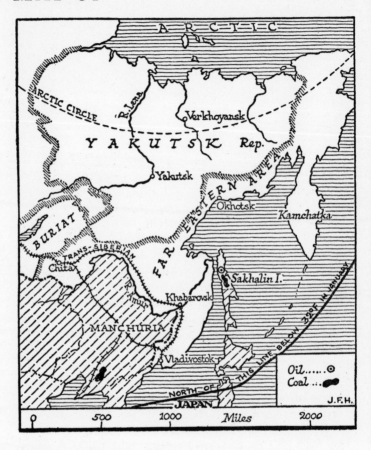

FAR EASTERN RUSSIA

THE FAR EAST of the Siberian territories of the U.S.S.R. is now politically divided into the Yakutsk republic, the largest in area, most sparsely populated, and least explored; and the Far Eastern Area, which includes the whole coast-line from the Arctic Ocean down to the port of Vladivostok, with Kamchatka and the northern part of the island of Sakhalin (the southern half of which is Japanese). Its administrative centre and military base is Khabarovsk, on the Amur river. So far—except in Sakhalin, where both coal and oil are worked—little has been done to exploit the known mineral wealth of the region.

It is this area, of course, whose security is threatened by the Japanese hold on Manchukuo. Its one link with the rest of Russia is the Trans-Siberian railway (*cf.* maps 50 and 51). The second Five-Year Plan includes schemes for extensive railway building in the Far Eastern Area, and the construction of a new port above Vladivostok.

MAP 62

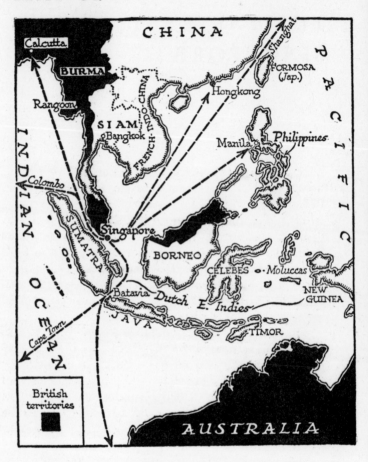

British territories

THE CROSS-ROADS OF THE FAR EAST: SINGAPORE

SINGAPORE, Britain's chief naval base in the Far East, stands at the western gateway to the Pacific Ocean—as Panama stands at its eastern entrance. The trade routes from India and Ceylon to China and Japan run through the Straits of Malacca, between the Malay Peninsula and the island of Sumatra (see also next map). When Sir Stamford Raffles annexed Singapore for Britain in 1819 he wrote—"It gives us the command of China and Japan, with Siam and Cambodia, to say nothing of the islands themselves."

The great naval dockyard now under construction there, at an estimated cost of £9,000,000, is to be completed in 1939. Naval experts regard it as essential for the protection of Australia and New Zealand, as well as of Hong-Kong and British commercial interests in China. Japan, on the other hand, naturally regards the fortification of Singapore as a menace to her expansion in Asia.

Most foreign commentators on international affairs assume that there is an understanding between Holland and Britain regarding the use of Singapore in case of any attack on the Dutch East Indies.

MAP 63

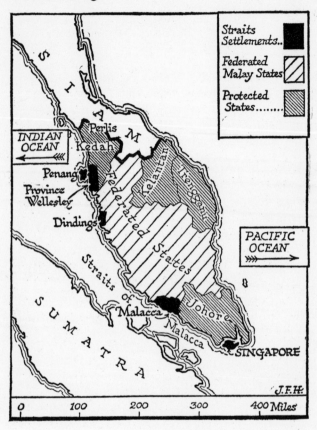

Straits Settlements.. ▪

Federated Malay States ▨

Protected States....... ▨

SIAM

INDIAN OCEAN

Perlis

Kedah

Penang

Province Wellesley

Dindings

Federated States

Kelantan

Trengganu

PACIFIC OCEAN

Straits of Malacca

SUMATRA

Malacca

Johore

Malacca

SINGAPORE

J.F.H.

0   100   200   300   400 Miles

BRITISH MALAYA

BRITISH INTEREST in the Malay Peninsula (which divides the Indian Ocean from the Pacific) began when the East India Company established a station at Penang before the end of the 18th century. A few years later Malacca, originally a Portuguese trading station, was taken over from the Dutch, and Stamford Raffles founded a British settlement at Singapore. British rule now extends over the whole peninsula south of the Siamese frontier; the five coast stations [1] —the Straits Settlements—forming one British Crown Colony, while the four Federated Malay States are subject to British suzerainty though ruled by nominally independent sultans, and the others are under British protection, with British advisers.

The extension of British control over the interior of the peninsula was due to the discovery, some 60 years ago, of rich tin deposits. At the beginning of the present century the production of rubber was commenced on a large scale and the result has been an industrial revolution which has put Malaya well into the modern world picture. Large numbers of Chinese and Indian workers were brought into the country for the mines and plantations, and these now outnumber the Malays. The hinterland of Singapore is therefore of very considerable economic importance, quite apart from the strategic value of the port itself.

[1] One of these, the Dindings, was retroceded to Perak, a Federated State, February, 1935.

MAP 64

British India ....

Indian States ....

KASHMIR

BALUCHISTAN

PATIALA

Delhi

NEPAL

BHUTAN

Indus

RAJPUTANA

Ganges

CUTCH

CENTRAL INDIA

Bhopal

KATHIAWAR

Baroda

Indore

ORISSA

Calcutta

(PORTUG.) Daman

Bombay

HYDERABAD

BASTAR

Yanam (FR.)

(PORTUGUESE) Goa →

MYSORE

Madras

Pondicherry

Karikal

} FRENCH

TRAVANCORE

J.F.H.

| 0 | 250 | 500 | 1000 | *Miles* | 1500 |

THE PROBLEM OF THE
INDIAN STATES

MOST PEOPLE, until the actual discussion of schemes of Indian self-government brought the question of the Indian States to the fore, vaguely assumed that India was uniformly under British control. Actually, of course, as the discussions have emphasised, the Indian peninsula is divided into British India, directly administered by the British Government of India, and a number of States, some of which enjoy full sovereign rights, others being subject to the "advisory jurisdiction" of the Government, while many smaller ones possess some degree of internal independence limited by a considerable measure of Government interference.

British India includes practically all the coast territories, as well as the valleys of the Ganges and the Indus. The States vary enormously not only in status and powers but in size, Kashmir and Hyderabad having areas of 84,000 and 82,000 square miles and populations of 3 million and 11¼ million respectively, while many of the smaller States comprise only a few acres.

N.B. In the map Nepal is shown within the Indian frontier. Actually it and the neighbouring small Buddhist State of Bhutan are independent allied states, both of which have agreed to conduct their external relations by the advice of the Government of India.

MAP 65

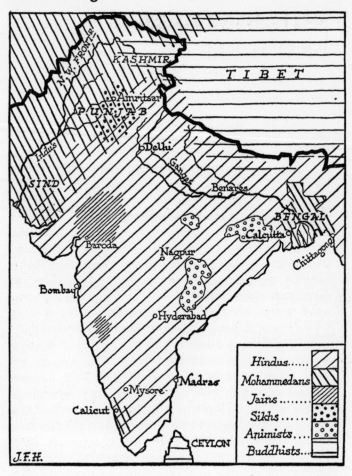

N.W. FRONTIER

KASHMIR

TIBET

Amritsar

PUNJAB

Delhi

Ganges

Benares

Indus

SIND

BENGAL

Calcutta

Baroda

Nagpur

Chittagong

Bombay

Hyderabad

Madras

Mysore

Calicut

CEYLON

J.F.H.

Hindus......	
Mohammedans	
Jains	
Sikhs	
Animists....	
Buddhists...	

INDIA:
THE COMMUNAL
PROBLEM

THE PROBLEM of religious minorities is another of the complications which the framers of a new constitution for India have had to face. Whether it is as complex as the opponents of self-government have always insisted may be open to question. Indian nationalists assert that it is a difficulty which would rapidly solve itself if Indians were left to look after their own affairs. The centre and south of the peninsula (*cf.* map) is predominantly Hindu. The great mass of Mahommedans are found in the north-west, in the Punjab and Sind, while another Mahommedan area is in lower Bengal. In the Punjab also are the Sikhs. Buddhism, which had its birthplace in India, is now only dominant over the frontier to the north-east in Tibet, and in Ceylon in the south. Indian nationalists, both Hindu and Mahommedan, are opposed to communal electorates, which, so they argue, would accentuate religious differences by making them into permanent political divisions.

MAP 66

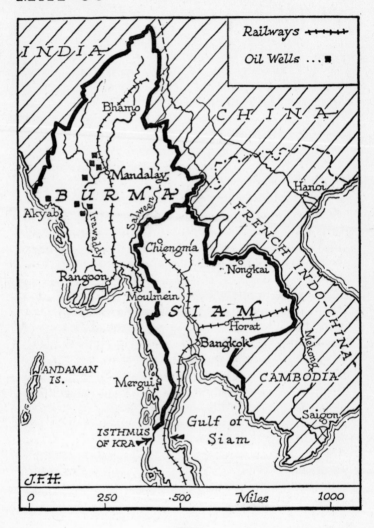

Railways ┼┼┼┼┼┼

Oil Wells ... ■

INDIA

CHINA

Bhamo

Mandalay

BURMA

Akyab

Irrawaddy

Salween

Hanoi

FRENCH INDO-CHINA

Chiengma

Nongkai

Rangoon

Moulmein

SIAM

Horat

Bangkok

ANDAMAN
IS.

Mergui

Mekong

CAMBODIA

Saigon

Gulf of
Siam

ISTHMUS
OF KRA

J.F.H.

| 0 | 250 | 500 | Miles | 1000 |

BURMA:
SIAM

Burma, although in tradition and culture a quite separate nation from India, was by the Government of India Act (1919) administered as part of British India. The rise and development of the Nationalist movement in India, however, has coincided with the growth in Burma of a separationist party, and by the new India Bill (1935) Burma is henceforth governed by a separate administration.

Geographically Burma is cut off from India by sea, mountain and jungle. Its land frontiers form a practically impassable barrier and its communications with India are by sea across the Bay of Bengal, Rangoon being 700 miles from Calcutta and 1,000 miles from Madras.

Siam, lying between Burma and French Indo-China, has during the past few years been the scene of various political upheavals, culminating in the abdication of King Prajadhipok (March 1935). It appears highly probable that these political changes are the result of the extensive economic penetration of Siam by Japan. Siamese foreign trade was up to a few years ago dominated by Great Britain and Singapore, but between 1931 and 1934 Japanese exports to Siam increased more than 500 per cent. It has been rumoured that Japan is ready to offer financial help to Siam for a canal across the Kra isthmus (see map), which would threaten the naval and economic dominance of Singapore.

MAP 67

TIBET

Tibet's geographical position in relation to India's northern frontier makes her government a matter of considerable concern to Britain. In 1903–4—at the time when the designs of Czarist Russia were still regarded in Britain with fear and suspicion—the British Government despatched a military expedition to the forbidden city of Lhasa and compelled the Tibetan Government to recognise special British interests. After the Chinese revolution (1911) China's suzerainty over Tibet was again asserted; but the recent breakdown of government in China enabled Britain, by negotiations with the late Dalai Lama to consolidate her influence. The spiritual head of Tibetan Buddhism, the Tashi Lama, who took over the Regency a year or two ago, had for some years been exiled in China, and his return to Tibet may be the signal for the renewal of the demand for Tibetan independence.

MAP 68

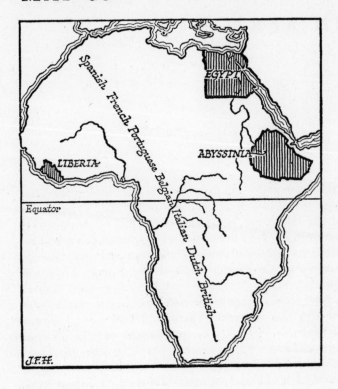

Spanish French Portuguese Belgian Italian Dutch British

EGYPT

ABYSSINIA

LIBERIA

Equator

J.F.H.

INDEPENDENT STATES
IN AFRICA

Since the great "scramble for Africa" took place during the last two decades of the 19th century the whole of the continent, with the exception of three areas, has been divided between the European Powers. The three states retaining some measure of independence —in each case strictly limited—are Egypt, Abyssinia and Liberia.

Ever since, in 1875, the British Government bought the Khedive's shares in the Suez Canal, the condition of affairs in Egypt has been a matter of primary concern to British Governments. On the outbreak of war in 1914 the nominal Turkish suzerainty over Egypt was ended and the country was made a British protectorate. After the War self-government was granted, but with important reservations. The Sudan remained under British control, British garrisons were to be maintained in the Canal Zone and at Cairo and Alexandria, and Egypt's foreign policy was to be guided by British interests.

For Abyssinia, see map 32.

For Liberia, see map 74.

MAP 69

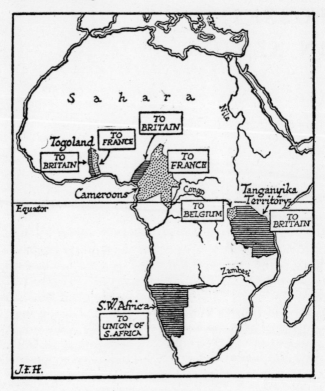

GERMANY'S LOST
POSSESSIONS
IN AFRICA

By the post-war Treaties all the German colonies in Africa were handed over, for the most part as mandates, to the victorious Powers. Togoland was divided between Britain and France, the British (western portion) now being administered with the Gold Coast. A small area of the Cameroons adjoining Nigeria went to Britain; the larger part went to France, part of it as a mandated territory, while the southern part was definitely ceded, becoming part of French Equatorial Africa. German East Africa, with the exception of a small area in the north-west which was added to the Belgian Congo, went to Britain, being re-named Tanganyika Territory. German South-West Africa, conquered during the War by the forces of the Union of South Africa, was handed over by mandate to the Union Government. The latter has taken steps to deal with Nazi organisations an propaganda in the territory.

MAP 70

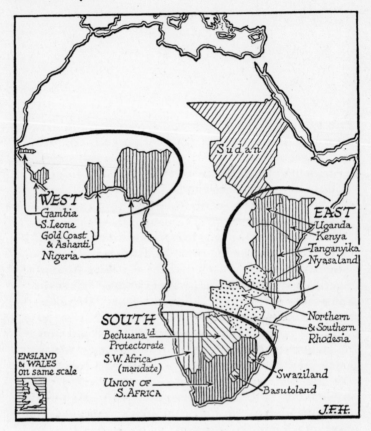

Sudan

WEST
Gambia
S. Leone
Gold Coast
& Ashanti
Nigeria

EAST
Uganda
Kenya
Tanganyika
Nyasaland

Northern
& Southern
Rhodesia

SOUTH
Bechuana ld
Protectorate
S.W. Africa
(mandate)
UNION OF
S. AFRICA

Swaziland
Basutoland

ENGLAND
& WALES
on same scale

J.F.H.

BRITAIN IN AFRICA

THE PRESENT CENTURY has seen a revolt on the part of various Asiatic peoples against European domination. There are many signs that that revolt will spread to Africa in the near future, and the spirit in which the various Colonial Powers handle the "native problem" will doubtless decide what form that revolt takes.

British possessions are spread over the length and breadth of the continent, presenting differing problems in different areas. British Africa may be conveniently classified (*cf.* map) into: (1) *West Africa*—Nigeria, and West Coast Colonies—where the main policy followed is that of Indirect Rule. There are no white settlers in this region. (2) *East Africa*, including Uganda, Kenya, Tanganyika and Nyasaland. In Tanganyika and Uganda an enlightened native policy prevails. In Kenya the presence of a considerable number of white settlers has complicated the problem (*cf.* later map). (3) *South Africa*, the territories included in the Union of South Africa, a self-governing dominion, with a native policy based on an absolute denial of the equality of races. Between South and East Africa lie the Rhodesias (*cf.* next map); and north of the East African territories, though geographically quite separate from them, is the British Sudan.

MAP 71

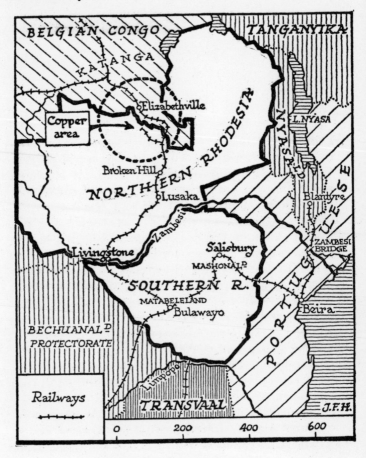

BELGIAN CONGO

TANGANYIKA

KATANGA

Copper area

Elizabethville

NORTHERN RHODESIA

Broken Hill

L. NYASA

NYASALAND

Lusaka

Zambesi

Blantyre

ZAMBESI BRIDGE

Livingstone

Salisbury

MASHONAL.D

PORTUGUESE

SOUTHERN R.

MATABELELAND

Bulawayo

Beira

BECHUANAL.D
PROTECTORATE

Railways

Limpopo

TRANSVAAL

J.F.H.

| 0 | 200 | 400 | 600 |

THE RHODESIAS

Northern and Southern Rhodesia were taken over by the British Government from the South African Chartered Company in 1923–4. Southern Rhodesia was at once granted a measure of "limited responsible government." Northern Rhodesia, at the time of the transfer possessing no very great economic value, has since become of first-class importance owing to the discovery of the great copper field (adjoining the Belgian Katanga field) which is estimated to be the richest in the world. "British Malaya," a recent writer has remarked, "saw the most striking example of an industrial revolution in the last generation—Northern Rhodesia promises to be the next."

The question of the native policy to be adopted during the development of such an area is likely to have repercussions far outside its own borders. To the north of it, both in the Belgian Congo and in Tanganyika, native interests are in various ways safeguarded against white exploitation. On the south, Rhodesia is in touch with the Union, where white interests are in every way paramount. A section of the North Rhodesian settlers is pressing for amalgamation with Southern Rhodesia, obviously in order to free themselves from British Parliamentary control.

MAP 72

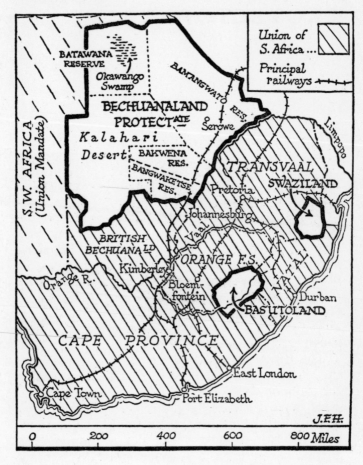

Union of
S. Africa...

Principal
railways

BATAWANA
RESERVE

Okawango
Swamp

BAMANGWATO RES.

BECHUANALAND
PROTECT^ATE

Kalahari
Desert

Serowe

BAKWENA
RES.

BANGWAKETSE
RES.

S.W. AFRICA
(Union Mandate)

TRANSVAAL

SWAZILAND

Limpopo

Pretoria

Johannesburg

Vaal

BRITISH
BECHUANA LD

Kimberley

ORANGE F.S.

Orange R.

Bloem-
fontein

BASUTOLAND

Durban

CAPE PROVINCE

East London

Cape Town

Port Elizabeth

J.F.H.

| 0 | 200 | 400 | 600 | 800 Miles |

THE SOUTH AFRICAN
PROTECTORATES

WHEN THE UNION OF SOUTH AFRICA was constituted in 1909 three British protectorates—Bechuanaland (not to be confused with British Bechuanaland, part of Cape territory), Basutoland, and Swaziland, remained directly under the control of the home government. The largest of them Bechuanaland, lies along the northern frontier of the Union. The two smaller ones are enclaves in Union territory. All three have suffered badly from administrative neglect during recent years, their treatment comparing very unfavourably with that of the West African colonies or Tanganyika.

The Union Government has made a demand for the transfer of the three territories to itself, basing the claim on a clause in the Act of Union which implied the inclusion of the Protectorates in the Union at some future date. Native opinion in the Protectorates is firmly opposed to the idea of transfer. The British Government has compromised by refusing actual transfer, but promising "closer economic co-operation" between the administration of the territories and the Union.

MAP 73

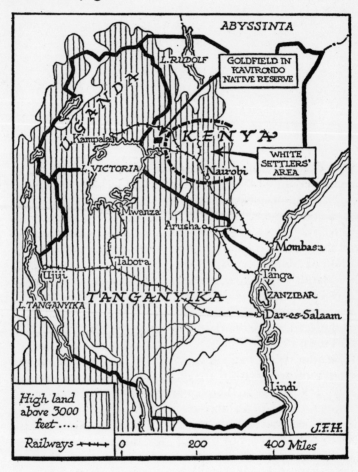

ABYSSINIA

L. RUDOLF

GOLDFIELD IN
KAVIRONDO
NATIVE RESERVE

U G A N D A

Kampala

L. VICTORIA

KENYA

WHITE
SETTLERS'
AREA

Nairobi

Mwanza

Arusha

Mombasa

Tabora

Tanga

ZANZIBAR

Ujiji

TANGANYIKA

Dar-es-Salaam

L. TANGANYIKA

Lindi

High land
above 3000
feet ....

Railways ←+++→

0   200   400 Miles

J.F.H.

146

BRITISH EAST AFRICA

As has been already noted, Tanganyika Territory, since Britain took over the mandate, has been administered on enlightened lines and is, in the Africa of to-day, a model of what alien rule can be. The history of Kenya Colony has been less fortunate. The building of the Uganda railway, connecting Uganda with the coast of Mombasa, led to the realisation that in the highlands in the west of Kenya white settlement was possible. This area comprises almost all the good land in the colony. The natives have been pushed out of it and placed in reserves, which even now are inadequate and must become more so as the population increases. The most recent happening in Kenya has been the discovery of gold within the Kavirondo native reserve near Lake Victoria. The Government's promise to the natives that on no account would the reserves be further encroached upon was promptly broken, and many square miles of territory thrown open to white concession hunters. The incident is of far more than local importance inasmuch as in every part of Africa to-day Africans are watching with critical eyes the behaviour of their white rulers.

MAP 74

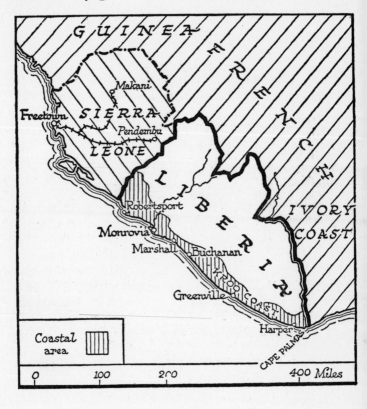

LIBERIA

The Colony of Liberia was founded in 1816, mainly through the efforts of the American Colonisation Society with the aim of settling free American negroes on African soil. In 1847 these negro colonists made a declaration of independence and established a republic. Civilisation, however, has never extended into the interior. Of the 50,000 more or less civilised inhabitants of the coastal region some 12,000 are of American origin. The population of the interior, variously estimated as from three-quarters of a million to 1½ millions, has been on occasion treated by its fellow African rulers in a way which can perhaps best be summarised as being a good imitation of the worst methods of white exploiters in other parts of the continent. Recent happenings led to a League of Nations enquiry and to a plan involving supervision of the Liberian Government by representatives of the League.

The United States has special interests in Liberia. In 1918 it advanced a loan to the republic and appointed a financial adviser. The economic resources of Liberia, moreover, are now largely mortgaged to the Firestone Rubber Co., of America, whose concession covers one million acres of land. There seems little doubt that the operations of the company, enforcing the plantation system on Liberia, have been in part responsible for the evils which the League of Nations plan seeks to eradicate.

INDEX

to places named in maps
All references in this index are to map numbers

ii

iii